BEYONCÉ

STERLING
New York

An Imprint of Sterling Publishing
387 Park Avenue South
New York, NY 10016

ISBN 978-1-4549-0365-9

Distributed in Canada by Sterling Publishing
c/o Canadian Manda Group, 165 Dufferin Street
Toronto, Ontario, Canada M6K 3H6
Distributed in the United Kingdom by GMC Distribution Services
Castle Place, 166 High Street, Lewes, East Sussex, England BN7 1XU
Distributed in Australia by Capricorn Link (Australia) Pty. Ltd.
P.O. Box 704, Windsor, NSW 2756, Australia

Produced for Sterling Publishing by Essential Works
www.essentialworks.co.uk

Publishing Director: Mal Peachey
Managing Director: John Conway
Editor: Nicola Hodgson

For information about custom editions, special sales, and premium and corporate purchases,
please contact Sterling Special Sales at 800-805-5489 or specialsales@sterlingpublishing.com.

Manufactured in China

2 4 6 8 10 9 7 5 3 1

www.sterlingpublishing.com

BEYONCÉ

ANDREW VAUGHAN

STERLING

New York

CONTENTS

INTRODUCTION

I n the spring of 2011 *Billboard* magazine, the music business bible, named Beyoncé Knowles as their artist of the millennium. It was a fitting reward for the Houston-born singer's sixteen Grammy awards, seventy-five million album sales around the world, hit movies, iconic music videos, and an exemplary life based on ideals and morals learned as a child in Texas.

It all began with Mathew Knowles, who like one of his idols in a previous era, Martin Luther King, had a dream. Both Beyoncé's parents grew up in pre–civil rights America and lived through some of the most dramatic changes in the social history of the United States, determined to partake of the American dream in every way possible.

Since the mid-1990s African Americans have had a remarkable role model in Oprah Winfrey, a phenomenally popular TV host and billionaire entrepreneur. In 2005, the year of America's terrible hurricane Katrina disaster in New Orleans, the U.S. Senate had just one black Senator, Barack Obama. Five years later he would be president. America was changing fast—something Mathew Knowles realized when he quit his job to launch his daughter's music career with Destiny's Child.

The Internet had revolutionized the music industry making the entertainment world more democratic and open than ever before and Knowles, more than anything, believed in the power of commitment and hard work. His daughter, Beyoncé, possessed two very rare talents. The first was an innate ability to sing and dance, but the other was probably more important. Beyoncé knew that talent alone was never enough. Practice, dedication, and sacrifice were every bit as important as raw talent. That she sits on top of the world today validates her sacrifices, even if she's sometimes wistful for the lost years of her childhood. "I was raised that anything that's worth anything takes a lot of sacrifice. And when anything is too easy for me I get scared."

Since the age of seven, Beyoncé has dedicated her life to the mastery of the entertainment craft. Her almost uninterrupted stream of success is the by-product of two decades of practice, focus, and commitment. Her music resumé is unparalleled: sixteen Grammy Awards, eleven Music

Opposite: The consummate performer, Beyoncé onstage in Los Angeles in 2009.

Television (MTV) Video Awards, and *Billboard's* Millennium Award. Beyoncé's movie career has also been a commercial success, with her six movies grossing $750 million.

Since the release of "Independent Women" Beyoncé has never stopped campaigning for the empowerment of women, inventing a new word, "bootylicious," in the process. She's championed numerous young artists and producers, taken charge of her own sound and been savvy enough to work with teams of the very best musical talents available to her. Her music has never stagnated, each album a progression in influences and styles.

More than that, during the era of pro-tools and lip-syncing, she has proved that a live performer can still rely on a powerful, beautiful voice as much as on tracks, loops, and stage theatrics.

And while she married another major pop star, Beyoncé has retained a rare dignity in the celebrity-obsessed 2000s, keeping a classy mystery to her marriage and private life.

Beyoncé is also a remarkable businesswoman. Together with her husband Jay-Z, she is part of one of the richest, most powerful couples in America. In fact, if it weren't for a certain couple called Obama, they'd be America's most powerful African-American husband and wife team. Not that the Obamas are threatened. The president has had the music of Beyoncé and Jay-Z on his iPod for years and had them play at his Inauguration ball.

Raised with a strong social conscience, Beyoncé has devoted time, energy, and money to giving back financially, using her power and wealth to help those who need it most. She's in control of her life, and one of the few in her position to understand the Internet age's immediacy and intrusion.

With a story so compelling and dramatic there have been ups and downs, and Beyoncé comes with some puzzling contradictions. She's part Sasha Fierce, flirting and grinding onstage, part conservative churchgoer. When interviewed she comes across as an open book and yet her life is a series of well-guarded secrets. She missed having a normal life and writes deeply personal songs, but casually talks about herself as a brand.

Maybe it's these fascinating contradictions, allied to a prodigious natural performer's talent and a remarkable work ethic in pop that makes Beyoncé Tina Knowles' story one of the most fascinating in popular music history.

Opposite: The singer entertaining the crowd at Earl's Court, London, in 1996.

ONE

SAY MY NAME

O N September 4, 1981, the beloved daughter of Célestine Ann Tina Beyincé and Mathew Knowles was born. She was christened Beyoncé (Giselle Knowles), her name inspired by the memory of Agnès Beyincé, the mother of Tina Knowles. Beyoncé explained the origins of her distinctive name to CNN's Larry King (broadcast April 23, 2009): "Well, my name, Beyoncé, is actually my mother's maiden name. Her last name is Beyincé. And there were no more men in the family, no more sons. So she said let me name my daughter, her first name, Beyoncé. And that's a little confusing enough. You know, growing up I was called 'Be-yownce' and 'Bounce' and 'Be-amichi.' And Beyoncé is easy enough."

Home was an affluent suburb of Houston, the largest city in Texas and epicenter of the U.S. oil industry. Houston may be the fourth-largest city in America, but it feels like a series of small cities. It's wonderfully diverse and multicultural, yet very Texan. It is down-home, ringing with southern hospitality, but at the same time sophisticated and artistic. Significantly for Beyoncé, Houston has a long legacy of musical diversity and innovation, from blues to Tex-Mex, psychedelic rock, ZZ Top, rap, hip-hop, and R & B.

The Knowleses were upper-middle class, and the young Beyoncé was fortunate to witness the importance of entrepreneurship and the value of hard work while she was growing up. Her father, a 1974 graduate of Fisk University (in Nashville, Tennessee) with a focus in economics and management, was an executive at Xerox. Her mother worked in a bank before she had Beyoncé. She later opened a hair salon, Headliners, on hip Montrose Avenue and it quickly became one of the top salons in Houston.

Born and raised in Galveston, she hadn't grown up in a privileged home. Tina Knowles later reflected on her humble beginnings: "Growing up, we were so poor I wondered how my parents could afford the tuition to send us to Catholic school. It wasn't until I was an adult that I found out my mom [a seamstress] had bartered her services." Like her daughters, Tina Knowles had a deep passion for music. She sang in a Supremes-influenced harmony group called the Veltones while in high school. A Motown fan, she loved the fashion as much as the music and, with some above-average seamstress skills, designed and made the group's outfits.

Mathew Knowles was raised in Alabama during the height of the civil rights movement. Interviewed for the Fox News special *Real American Stories*, he remembered being "one of the first African Americans at Litchfield Junior High. Having state troopers take me to school every day. Having parents outside with signs and saying very negative things about a young kid."

Mathew also had an affinity for music and a desire to follow in the footsteps of Motown mogul Berry Gordy. He told Fox News: "I always had a dream for myself. I had always given myself twenty years in corporate America. I wanted to be in the music industry. It was happening at the same time that my oldest daughter, Beyoncé, had a dream that she wanted to be in the music industry."

Above: The superstar as a baby.

Opposite: Beyoncé with her sister Solange, to whom she has always been close, in 2003.

FIRST TALENT SHOW

ROM early childhood, Beyoncé showed an interest in music. She constantly sang and danced around the house and when she was just five years old was taken to see Michael Jackson in concert. It was an event that she later claimed set her on her musical journey. Beyoncé told Molly Meldrum of Australia's Channel 7 show *Sunday Night*, "I was—how old was I, five years old? It was my first concert and it was his show. And that night, I decided exactly my purpose."

Problem was, Beyoncé was an extremely shy child. To help her come out of her shell, her parents enrolled her in after-school dance classes at her elementary school, St. Mary's. The teacher, Darlette Johnson, would have a profound effect on Beyoncé, recognizing a raw talent and then encouraging the painfully shy child to utilize her gifts.

Interviewed on *The Ellen DeGeneres Show*, Darlette recalled the moment when she first heard Beyoncé sing. "She was at the studio and she was the last one and her parents always came to get her, to pick her up, and I was just kinda sweeping around . . . and I was singing a song out of tune and Beyoncé finished the song for me and she hit a note and I said, 'Sing it again.' She was a very shy girl. She was maybe about six or seven and her parents came to pick her up. I said, 'She can sing! She really can sing.' They let me put her in some singing competitions and dance competitions and it's been history since."

Nobody was more surprised to see Beyoncé win her first talent show than her father. She was the youngest contestant in the show and sang John Lennon's wistful "Imagine." She received a standing ovation and took home first prize.

Her father, Mathew Knowles, recalled the event to *Billboard* magazine in 2009, "She got up onstage and when she was finished, she received a standing ovation. Her mother and I looked at each other and said, 'That can't be our Beyoncé. She's shy and quiet.'"

Hooked on singing, Beyoncé quickly joined the choir at her family's church, St. John's United Methodist Church, often performing as a soloist when there wasn't a talent show to enter. "She must have done thirty of those competitions," her father remembered in an interview with *Ebony* magazine in 2001. "And she carried first place in every last one of them."

In 1988, Beyoncé received her first press with a mention in the *Houston Chronicle* following her nomination for the Sammy, a prestigious Houston arts award.

The following year Beyoncé enrolled at the Cynthia Ann Parker Elementary School, a Houston music magnet school whose mission statement was "to develop knowledge and character one child at a time." Embracing her love of music, Beyoncé received vocal coaching for one hour a day on top of her other lessons.

Above: A young Beyoncé in a school yearbook photo in around 1996.
Opposite: The polished performer in 2004.

MARIAH CAREY

Eight-year-old Beyoncé was just discovering her voice and about to start at Parker Elementary when a brand-new female singing star emerged. Mariah Carey's debut hit, "Vision of Love," was all over TV in the summer of 1990. Appearances on *Tonight* and *Arsenio Hall* allowed the twenty-year-old Long Islander to run through the stupendous range of her voice live, in front of millions of people. An a capella version performed live on *Good Morning America* in September 1990 was breathtaking in its execution and confirmed that here was a truly gifted singer.

The video for the single, with Mariah seated in front of a beautiful gothic window in a church, must have had huge appeal for the Methodist choir singer Beyoncé that summer of 1990. The vast range of Carey's voice and the fact that she was using it on a pop song, not a gospel (or operatic) number, can only have given Beyoncé hope for a future in the entertainment business.

It had taken Mariah Carey only two years to go from hawking a four-song demo tape to record company offices in Manhattan to international singing star. After Columbia Records boss Tommy Mottola met the singer, having heard her tape in his limo, he signed her to the label and started working to turn her into a marketable product. After "Vision of Love" made it to the top spot on record charts in America, Mottola was reported as stating, "When I heard and saw Mariah, there was absolutely no doubt that she was in every way destined for superstardom."

> ## "The vast range of Carey's voice and the fact that she was using it on a pop song . . . can only have given Beyoncé hope for a future in the entertainment business."

"Vision of Love" went on to earn Mariah Grammy Award nominations for Record of the Year and Song of the Year in 1991 and wins for Best New Artist and Best Female Pop Vocal Performance. The debut album received rave reviews and made the number one spot on the *Billboard* Hot 100 chart after Mariah's appearance and victories at the 1991 Grammys. In September of the same year, her second album, *Emotions*, was released, and the title track, the first single taken from the collection, reached number one—it was her fourth consecutive top hit. Early in 1992 Mariah performed seven songs on *MTV Unplugged* (including the old Jackson 5 number "I'll Be There"), reminding everyone that she was not just a manufactured pop star, but a truly great singer.

In 1993, just as Beyoncé was getting serious about Girl's Tyme, Carey married Tommy Mottola and released *Music Box*, her third album. The album contained a cover version of an old song that Nilsson had scored a huge international hit with in 1972, "Without You." Mariah's version was released in January 1994, and became her biggest-selling international hit single. The release of 1994's *Merry Christmas* (the best-selling Christmas album ever) saw her successfully cross over from R & B to mainstream pop star. Her fourth album, *Daydream* (1995), continued that move away from hip-hop and R & B music, and it quickly became her biggest-selling (non-seasonal) album release. Her singing style remains an influence on upcoming artists to this day.

Opposite: Mariah Carey, a star who has influenced every generation since she burst onto the music scene in 1990.

"I GREW UP IN A VERY NICE HOUSE IN HOUSTON, WENT TO PRIVATE SCHOOL ALL MY LIFE AND I'VE NEVER EVEN BEEN TO **THE 'HOOD.** NOT THAT THERE'S ANYTHING WRONG WITH THE 'HOOD."

Gospel and church music played a major role in Beyoncé's early life. Her parents played gospel music in the house, as she later recalled to iVillage: "I grew up listening to Ann Nesby and Shirley Caesar, and they have influenced so many of the people who I like." Beyoncé would later work with both these gospel legends in the movie *The Fighting Temptations*. More contemporary gospel artists like Yolanda Adams and Kim Burrell had taken the world by storm with their contemporary, jazz-influenced performances, and Beyoncé soaked it all up. At a more local level, church was a cornerstone of the Knowleses' family life. Beyoncé told *Entertainment Weekly* how important St. John's Methodist United Church, where she sang in the choir, was to her development. "You can be sitting next to a recovering alcoholic or a homeless person, but we're all the same . . . we're there to get the same thing."

Soul greats Anita Baker and Luther Vandross filled the Knowles household and her mother's salon while Beyoncé was growing up. As she recounted to *Entertainment Weekly*, "My mother played her and Luther Vandross all day at her hair salon. I always performed her music when I made my mom's friends watch me sing."

One singer who stood out in terms of technical influence was jazz singer Rachelle Ferrell. She had started out as a backing vocalist to Lou Rawls, Patti LaBelle, Vanessa Williams, and George Duke in the 1970s and released a series of jazz albums in the 1990s that heavily influenced Beyoncé's singing style. As Beyoncé told *Entertainment Weekly*: "My voice teacher listened to her; that's what I'd sing during my voice lessons. She uses her voice like an instrument."

And then there was the Houston hip-hop scene. As a resident of the Third Ward, a district in southeast Houston, Beyoncé had an early exposure to hip-hop. The center of Houston's African-American community, "the Trey"—as the Third Ward is referred to in rap circles—was the home of "chopped and screwed" music.

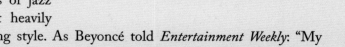

"I SACRIFICED SO MUCH AS A KID AND AS A TEENAGER, I HAVE NO REGRETS BECAUSE MY JOB KEPT ME FOCUSED."

Above: Beyoncé presenting an award to one of her idols Michael Jackson in 2003.

This was a style created by DJ Screw in the 1990s when he slowed down the beat and chopped up the original in the remix. In Houston, rappers like Scarface, Willie D, and Bushwick Bill (of the Geto Boys) surfaced while Beyoncé was growing up. Hip-hop played a key role in her early musical partnership with LaTavia Roberson, a dancer whom she'd met at an audition at the age of eight while attending the People's Workshop for the Visual and Performing Arts, an annual event spawned by Texas Southern University. The duo soon began to rap and sing together at local events.

Where an artist's understanding and manipulation of the record business was concerned, Beyoncé has talked often about the role Madonna played in inspiring her back when she was figuring out how the industry worked and how best to apply herself to becoming a star. Perhaps even more importantly, Michael Jackson too was a favorite performer and, as she got older, he became a role model in terms of work ethic and discipline. She later recalled her first concert to Australia's *Sunday Night* TV show: "He's the reason I do what I do, because I would have never experienced that magic if it wasn't for him." Michael Jackson passed away in the summer of 2009. At the next Grammy Awards he was presented with the Grammy Lifetime Achievement Award, and the day after, Beyoncé appeared on *The Tyra Banks Show* and told host Tyra Banks about the King of Pop's effect on her life. "I'm so happy I got to tell him on numerous occasions how much he impacted my life and I honestly would not have been anything, I mean, any success I've had I wouldn't have had without Michael Jackson. He's taught me so much and my family so much."

TWO

GIRL'S TYME

AUDITIONS AND
STAR SEARCH

BY 1990 Beyoncé had already begun performing with LaTavia Roberson. Her showmanship and onstage presence caught the eye of Andretta Tillman, a Houston entrepreneur, who was in the midst of auditioning talent for a girl group she was creating. Teen groups were big business at the time; New Kids on the Block were massive and En Vogue had just burst out of California. When she saw Beyoncé at the People's Workshop, Tillman wanted her in the group. It was to be called Girl's Tyme, and Tillman auditioned more than forty girls before selecting Beyoncé Knowles, LaTavia Roberson, Tamar Davis, and sisters Nikki and Nina Taylor. Kelly Rowland, who had been introduced to Beyoncé by Latavia, would join the group shortly afterward. As Latavia later recalled to MTV, "I met Beyoncé in 1990, when I was eight years old, at auditions for a local group in Houston. They wanted it to be all different races, they just wanted it to be a big group. And there were a lot of girls—I mean a lot of girls—but out of sixty five girls, Beyoncé and I made it. I met Kelly in elementary school a year later, and Beyoncé and LeToya were in middle school."

Not surprisingly, Mathew and Tina Knowles were actively involved in supporting Girl's Tyme from the beginning, organizing the girls and giving them rehearsal space at Tina's hair salon. They knew how much this meant to their daughter and were prepared to help in any way they could to ensure the success of the group.

With time, the local buzz began to swirl around the six young girls. On August 18, 1992, the *Houston Chronicle* spotlighted the group in a feature and referenced their mixing of "rap" flows and R & B "vocals." The following year, Girl's Tyme would make its national debut on *Star Search* (a predecessor to *American Idol*). During the group's introduction, the host—Ed McMahon—would refer to the young ladies as "the hip-hop rapping Girl's Tyme."

LaTavia opened the performance with a spirited rap, while Beyoncé took command of lead vocals as the other members danced in the background. In spite of the group's lively performance, they would lose the competition to rock band Skeleton, which received a perfect score from the judges. With hindsight as a guide, it was obvious that hip-hop had not yet sustained enough of a hold over mainstream American audiences for them to vote for this style of music.

The girls were distraught at their loss, but Mathew Knowles's reaction was more considered. Instead of wallowing in disappointment, he asked the show's producers for advice. He was told that the losing acts often went on to gain the most by learning from their mistakes. With that, Knowles knew it was time for him to get more involved in the group. They needed direction, and his time, like Beyoncé's, was about to come. He told *Ebony* magazine in 2001, "That's where I developed my concept, from Berry Gordy. He doesn't get the credit he deserves. He had everything in-house. He had his choreographers, stylists, producers, and writers. He taught his artists etiquette. He had real artist development. And his artists were glamorous. That's really what the music world is all about."

Opposite: From left to right, LeToya Luckett, Kelly Rowland, Beyoncé, and LaTavia Roberson pose as Girl's Tyme in 1998. They would later be known to the world as Destiny's Child.

ARTIST management was the next step for Mathew Knowles. He'd already established a company, Music World Entertainment, while working full-time in sales, and now it was time for him to emulate his music-biz role models, Berry Gordy at Motown and the Jacksons' father-manager, Joe. Knowles enrolled in music-business classes at a local community college in Houston and turned one of the family's bedrooms into an office.

Gathering information fast and utilizing the marketing skills and business savvy he'd cultivated from previous work experiences, Knowles worked tirelessly with Andretta Tillman to turn Girl's Tyme into a hit act. He threw himself into the project, learning as he went. "I had to be the front sound man, I had to be the security, I had to be the road manager, I had to wear all of those hats, and so it allowed me to really understand almost every aspect of the day-to-day."

Girl's Tyme shrunk to a trio of Beyoncé, Kelly, and LaTavia—when Tamar Davis and the Taylor sisters departed—but they were then joined by LeToya Luckett. The four-member group gelled immediately, musically and personally, which made the rigors of what Mathew Knowles called "boot camp" bearable, indeed enjoyable.

The girls went running, worked out every day, rehearsed constantly, worked on choreography, and took voice lessons from renowned opera singer and vocal coach David Lee Brewer.

"THE FOUR-MEMBER GROUP GELLED IMMEDIATELY"

Knowles organized more intense activities during the summer vacations. Family friend Vernell Jackson recalled their hard work to *The Observer* in 2001: "There was a lot of stuff they had to sacrifice, and that was basically the friendships that they would have formed outside. But they were determined. And people think that parents push your child to do this, but Mathew and Tina weren't ever like that. The way they were was, 'My daughter wants to do it, and this is the one thing that she wants to do.'"

Mathew Knowles was tough on the girls; they were, after all, only ten and eleven years old. "I believe in setting goals and getting the job done, and having everybody understand that this is where we've got to go," he told *Ebony* magazine in 2001.

Not that the girls were complaining. They were doing what they loved, and Beyoncé in particular had obviously inherited her parents' work ethic, as Vernell Jackson noted: "Beyoncé particularly always had that thing about, 'I want to do it right.' She wanted to work on it, like her singing and her voice lessons and her dancing. She always wanted to be maybe like Janet Jackson or Michael Jackson—those type of people."

Above: Destiny's Child in 1990.

For her part, Tina worked long hours at the salon to make up for the loss of her husband's wages and devoted any spare time she had to working with the girls on hair, makeup, and costumes.

Not that it was plain sailing—far from it. Financially, the family took a battering and the pressures put a strain on Tina and Mathew's marriage, as Tina explained to *Teen Hollywood* in 2003: "Mathew would spend $5,000 of our money on a photo shoot, while I was working sixteen hours a day to support us. I felt like the group was more important to him than his family. So we separated for six months. But we were miserable apart. We got back together and never let money separate us again."

TLC

At the beginning of the 1990s, gangsta rap was the hardest, edgiest, hippest sound around in L.A. New jack swing, a soulful, house-music-inspired R & B style, dominated the East Coast teen club scene and supplied the soundtrack for a new wave of black-powered cinema releases of the day (*New Jack City, Juice, House Party, Boyz n the Hood*). The sounds of rap and new jack swing shared attitudes of resistance, belligerence, and funky joy. Both mixed samples from old-school soul, funk, and disco records of the 1960s and 1970s, using James Brown's funky drummer beat, Rick James's bass lines, and Sly Stone's horn breaks behind semi-sung, semi-rapped messages about life lived on the street.

To a musically precocious ten-year-old like Beyoncé, new jack swing must have been the only rhythm and attitude to adopt. Mariah Carey's vocal range had shown her that she was allowed to sing across the range, but the success of a brand-new all-female group called TLC (which was most definitely not an acronym for "tender loving care") showed Beyoncé and Girl's Tyme the way forward to success. TLC—named after members Tionne "T-Boz" Watkins, Lisa "Left Eye" Lopes, and Rozonda "Chilli" Thomas—wore fun, colorful, oversized clothes, their hair under kerchiefs, and what looked like a condom as an eye patch (it was). Their sassy half-rapped songs were unlike anything that you'd hear from the Supremes or Vanity 6.

New jack swing depended on the mixing and production skills of producers for its special sound

> **"The success of a brand-new all-girl group called TLC showed Beyoncé and Girl's Tyme the way forward to success."**

and success. Jimmy Jam and Terry Lewis, fresh from Prince's Minneapolis music collective the Time, would soon make a big star out of Janet Jackson (see pages 80–81). Teddy Riley would coproduce Michael Jackson's *Dangerous*, having enjoyed recording success as part of Guy. Kenneth "Babyface" Edmonds had produced Bobby Brown and Paula Abdul in the 1980s and in 1989 set up LaFace Records with fellow producer L.A. Reid—who in 1991 signed TLC to the label.

TLC's debut album, *Oooooooohhh...On the TLC Tip* was released in February 1992, having been preceded by the first single taken from it, "Ain't 2 Proud 2 Beg." Released in November 1991, the single would make the top ten in the United States and earn Lisa "Left Eye" Lopes a Grammy nomination as cowriter (with Dallas Austin) for Best R & B Song.

The album was a showpiece for each member's particular musical style. Beyoncé must have noticed that T-Boz did the funky songs, Left Eye rapped, and Chilli took an R & B stand. Each member was individually defined as her own person, with her own "thing" that she was into. Unfortunately for Left Eye, that "thing" turned out to be alcohol fueled, and by the time of the second album (*CrazySexyCool*) early in 1994, she was under a five-year probation sentence. Despite the success of a third album, *FanMail* (1999), the group fell apart. By that time, though, they were also facing a new musical competitor—an all-female R & B trio named Destiny's Child had arrived on the scene in a big way.

Opposite: Lisa "Left Eye" Lopes, Rozonda "Chilli" Thomas, and Tionne "T-Boz" Watkins of TLC.

SIGNING A DEAL AND
FACING REJECTION

"**T**HE key thing was always their passion," Mathew Knowles told *Billboard* magazine in 2006. "This wasn't a parent or manager putting together a group to see about getting a record deal. This was young girls saying, 'This is what we want.'"

With tireless determination, the group rehearsed feverishly and performed anywhere they could—from corporate meetings to fashion shows and church functions.

You don't become a top corporate salesman without learning how to get people's attention, and Mathew Knowles was never shy about talking up his act. Relentlessly pursuing record companies to take notice of his talented brood, he was able to spark some interest, and record company representatives began to check out the girls' performances. Knowles got Girl's Tyme an audition with Columbia Records, and they performed in front of the label's Teresa LaBarbera (who would play a key role later in their career).

It didn't go well, as Mathew Knowles explained to *Ebony* in 2001: "I remember when I had Columbia Records come in to see them audition when they were twelve. The day before, I told the girls not to get in the swimming pool, that they would get congested. They didn't listen to me. In the middle of the audition, I stopped and told them: 'This is exactly what I was talking about. You guys decided to go swimming, and now you are not sounding good.'"

Fortunately for Beyoncé and Co., the group was being noticed, and one performance at Houston's Black Expo drew the attention of Daryl Simmons at Silent Partner Productions in Atlanta. Simmons, especially impressed with Beyoncé's vocal prowess, tipped off Elektra's Sylvia Rhone (who had signed En Vogue while at Atlantic Records). Rhone was CEO and president of Elektra and had recently been credited as "the most powerful woman in the music business" by the *Los Angeles Times*.

The deal with Elektra set the girls up with Simmons (Babyface's partner) and L.A. Reid, who was one of the hottest producers in pop music at that time. L.A. Reid and Simmons were based in Atlanta, so Girl's Tyme and family relocated to Georgia for the duration of the album. LaTavia Roberson's mother acted as chaperone, and various parents and family members took turns staying with the girls in their new temporary Atlanta home. The girls had a good time, but the recording sessions were not impressing the record company. Frustratingly, after eight months the company decided that Beyoncé and Co. were not yet ready for the big time and dropped them from the label. The girls dealt with the rejection as they had with their *Star Search* loss. There was initial disappointment followed by a determination to improve and prove to the powers that be that they had made a huge mistake.

Above: Girl's Tyme in 1992.
Opposite: A four-piece Destiny's Child making an appearance in London, 1998.

"THERE'S A LINE
BETWEEN SEXY AND NASTY,
AND DESTINY'S CHILD IS

SEXY,

YES WE ARE, BUT WE'RE

NEVER NASTY."

REACHING FOR
DESTINY

THE name had to go. Girl's Tyme seemed to be bringing the girls bad luck as they tried to further their singing career. Inspired by a quote from Isaiah 11:6, the group came up with a new name—Destiny's Child—a change that seemed to help bring about the success they had been looking for. The Book of Isaiah was one of Tina Knowles's favorites, and she had slipped a picture of the group into her Bible as a bookmark. Kelly Rowland told the rest of the story to *Black Beat Magazine* in 1998: "Beyoncé's mom was reading the Bible one day and at the time we were looking for a name. And she was looking in the Book of Isaiah, and right up under the word 'destiny' was a picture of us. We are very much Christians and we totally believe and have faith in God. And we believe that He sent us that name. We used the name for a little while, but we found out that other groups had it. And we tried to switch it up, so we made it Destiny's Child."

The name change refreshed the girls, and they began to pick up gigs supporting major acts who played in Houston. Meanwhile, Mathew Knowles stuck at his task and went back to Columbia Records, for whom they had already auditioned poorly. Columbia had the girls fly to New York to sing for them in the company's conference room. This time around they weren't interested in seeing a Destiny's Child song-and-dance routine. Instead, the trio were asked to perform Bill Withers's "Ain't No Sunshine" and one original a cappella. It was all about the voices.

It was weeks before Knowles heard back from Columbia. Destiny's Child had a record deal. Beyoncé was ecstatic. Three years after the disappointment of *Star Search*, they not only had a recording deal; they now shared a label with Michael Jackson, Céline Dion, and Mariah Carey. Ironically, while Elektra, a forty-year-old company with a reputation for the eclectic and adventurous had rejected the group, it was the historic and all-powerful Columbia Records that had faith in Girl's Tyme. Not only was Columbia one of America's most revered record companies, with a history of classic music dating back to 1887, but it had recently been purchased by Sony, and was probably the most powerful entertainment company in the world.

Mathew Knowles was still co-managing the band with Andretta Tillman, but Knowles wanted the girls all to sign with his Music World Entertainment management company. There were some reservations about this deal from Roberson's and Luckett's parents, but perhaps recognizing that Knowles possessed the tenacity and determination to make things happen, they all signed. Columbia made Destiny's Child a priority and assigned Mariah Carey's publicist to the group for media training and publicity guidance.

Everything seemed as though it was coming together nicely, but just when things were looking rosy, Destiny's Child faced tragedy. Andretta Tillman, who had put the girls together all those years earlier, became seriously ill with lupus, a fairly uncommon and complex autoimmune disease. Andretta died in 1997 after a long struggle with the illness. But the girls didn't forget her, honoring Andretta with dedications on their first three albums.

Opposite: The girls at the 1998 MTV European Music Awards.
Following pages: Destiny's Child performing in 2000.

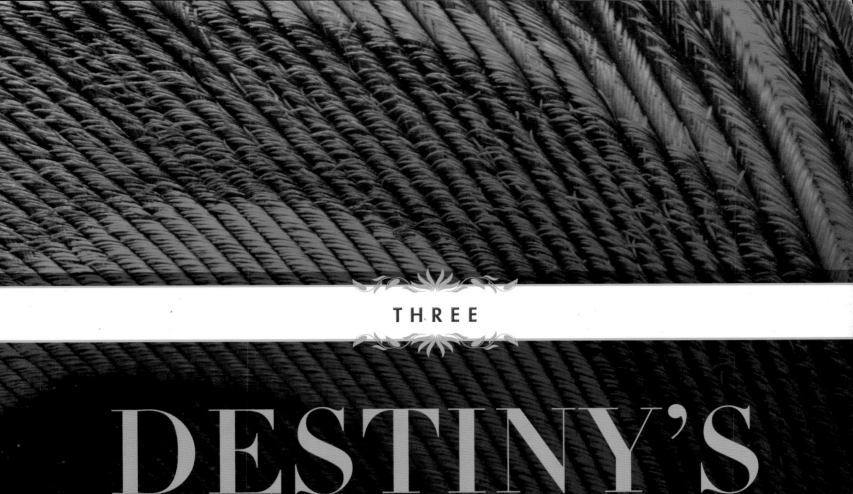

THREE

DESTINY'S CHILD

THE WORLD MEETS
DESTINY'S CHILD

ESTINY's Child could hardly complain about their big break in America and their introduction to audiences worldwide. The newly signed group's first recording, "Killing Time," was featured on the sound track for the 1997 release *Men in Black*. The big-budget sci-fi movie was a box office blockbuster, and the accompanying album followed suit, hitting the top spot on the *Billboard* album chart that July. "Killing Time" was deftly produced by D'Wayne Wiggins—a founding member of Tony! Toni! Toné! with five number one hits to his credit. It was a melodic, low-key affair that perfectly fitted the changing sound of R & B with its blend of soul, gospel, and pop—and just a hint of the power of Beyoncé's vocals.

If placement on a major movie sound track was the kind of favor a multinational record company could arrange for a new act, Destiny's Child, in return, was ready to compete professionally at the very highest level. The years of dedication and hard work with constant rehearsal, training, lessons, and absorbing everything Mathew Knowles had taught them were about to set the girls apart from all the other new acts in the business.

Sony Urban Music president Lisa Ellis recalled—in conversation with *Billboard* magazine—the group's first radio promo show for radio station WJJS in Roanoke, Virginia: "They were in a parking lot in front of a department store on a one-foot riser with a stage. Yet those girls came prepared like they were playing Madison Square Garden. They were doing their own hair and makeup, complete with costume changes. Tina literally sewed all the clothes back then. There were no lights or cameras. Just them and a crowd of people. And they killed it."

On November 11, 1997, Destiny's Child released their first single—"No No No"—which was divided into two parts: a charming swing-beat ballad produced by Rob Fusari and Vincent Herbert (Part 1) and a dance club remix produced by Wyclef Jean (Part 2).

Jean's remix came late in the day, the record company wanting something hip and punchy that would grab the listeners' attention for Destiny's Child's debut single. Jean took the original track, sped it up significantly, and threw in a sample of the Love Unlimited Orchestra's "Strange Games and Things."

"No No No (Part 2)" swiftly rose up the charts—hitting number one on *Billboard*'s R & B chart and number three on the Hot 100 chart and making the top five in the United Kingdom. Wyclef Jean rapped at the end of the song that Destiny's Child "went from a dream to the young Supremes." The Supremes name check was quite a compliment. It was a comparison that would follow Destiny's Child and Beyoncé for years to come.

"No No No" had built nicely on the success of their *Men in Black* sound track song. The future of Destiny's Child was looking very bright. The next step was to record and release their first album, which would be the stepping stone to the even greater stardom that they had been working toward since childhood.

Opposite: Kelly Rowland, LaTavia Roberson, Beyoncé Knowles, and LeToya Luckett at the
Soul Train Awards in 1998, where they were nominated for Best Group.

"THERE WERE NO

LIGHTS OR CAMERAS.

JUST THEM AND A CROWD OF

PEOPLE. AND THEY KILLED IT."

DESTINY'S Child's self-titled debut album was produced primarily by D'Wayne Wiggins, who had signed the girls to his Grass Roots Entertainment production company in 1995, before their Columbia Records deal. Wiggins had been a founding member of Tony! Toni! Toné!, who had sold more than six million albums between 1988 and 1996.

Faced with the challenge of producing age-appropriate material for the young women of Destiny's Child, Wiggins struck a delicate balance that celebrated their youth—adding just a sprinkle of sass—without making them appear childish. Despite having sixteen producers working on the album, all trying to find the right musical voice for Destiny's Child, the record is remarkably cohesive.

It was Wyclef Jean's involvement in the project that gave the new girl group the cutting edge necessary to stand apart from the crowd. In 1997, Jean was riding high as a producer/writer/collaborator thanks to the phenomenal commercial and critical success of the Fugees. Named in the top ten of hip hop groups of all time by MTV, the Fugees featured Wyclef Jean, fellow Haitian and rapper Pras Michel, along with Lauryn Hill. The group effortlessly fused soul, hip hop, and reggae into a cool unique sound. They had set the charts alight in 1995 with a stunning version of Roberta Flack's "Killing Me Softly with His Song." After a chance encounter with Destiny's Child in New York, he asked the girls to sing on his track "We Trying to Stay (Alive.") The girls then asked Jean to work with them on a different version of "No No No."

"WORKING WITH DESTINY'S CHILD WAS INCREDIBLE. WE SEE THE POTENTIAL."

Jean told *Mixonline.com*: "Working with Destiny's Child was incredible. We see the potential. In the line of work we are in, you can see who's gonna blow and who's not gonna blow. And what I loved about Beyoncé and Kelly the most—when I worked with them in the studio—is their attitudes: humble, they laid-back. And that's the attitude that determines how long you're really gonna last in this thing."

Not only did Jean encourage the girls to experiment vocally in the studio, helping them develop their trademark staccato delivery; he also played a key role in creating their image. The day of the video shoot for "No No No (Part 2)" saw the group without costumes. Their luggage had been lost somewhere between the United

Above: The release of Destiny's Child's debut album was the springboard to huge success around the world, including winning the MOBO award for best International R&B Act.

States and Cancún, Mexico, where they were shooting a video. Fortunately, Tina Knowles was with them on that trip and, as she had done for years, set about making costumes for the video. She found a local army surplus store, jazzed up some military outfits, and won Jean's approval—he told Tina she should always be in charge of the group's costumes.

While most new acts would have been overjoyed at their launch on the world stage, Beyoncé and her fellow members of Destiny's Child were not satisfied. "The first record was successful but not hugely successful," Beyoncé told the British newspaper *The Guardian*. "It was a neo-soul record and we were fifteen years old. It was way too mature for us." That drive to improve and deliver the album they knew they had in them would surface on the next recording—that would be their breakthrough album *The Writing's on the Wall*.

MISSY ELLIOTT

Born Melissa Elliott to an abusive Marine father in 1971, Missy lived in a trailer and a run-down slum in Virginia until the age of fourteen. She grew up tough and was determined to be a singer or entertainer of some sort. Her talent, determination, and incredible skill as a producer made her an obvious influence on Beyoncé, even before the two worked together on Destiny Child's "Get on the Bus" in 1998. After making the acquaintance of Jodeci's DeVante Swing, Missy moved to New York along with her band, Fayze, and their producer, Timothy Mosely, in 1991. Fayze signed to his Swing Mob label (distributed via Elektra) and were renamed Sista. Swing Mob include Ginuwine, Playa, and Tweet, and they, along with Missy and her friend Mosely, now renamed Timbaland, made music, produced, and jammed together, all while living in the same house. In 1995, with Sista not having released any songs or albums and Swing Mob folded, Missy and Timbaland moved on to work together, writing songs and producing. They put together most of Aaliyah's sophomore album, *One in a Million*, in 1996.

The success of *One in a Million* (which sold more than two million copies) made Missy and Timbaland the most wanted producers in New York City, which is how they eventually got to work with Beyoncé. The remarkable success of Missy Elliott as a producer is notable not only because she was operating in a predominantly masculine environment, but also because she began a successful recording career as she produced for others. Her debut album, *Supa Dupa Fly*, was recorded in a week and released in 1997, propelled by the hit single "The Rain." The album sold a million copies and made Missy an international star.

Despite Missy not looking or sounding like the contemporary R & B divas of the time (Mariah, Janet, Mary J. Blige), she went from sales strength to strength with successive album releases over a five-year period. *Da Real World* (1999) sold three million copies worldwide (and had taken a whole two months to record). *Miss E...So Addictive* (2001) included the international hit singles "One Minute Man" (featuring Ludacris) and "Get Ur Freak On" and reached the number two spot on the *Billboard* Hot 200 album chart (number one on the R & B chart). *Under Construction* (2002), however, was her most successful album. Drawing on old-school rap and funk sounds, she and Timbaland created what the *New York Times* called "this year's best hiphop album." In 2003 Missy, Mc Flyte, and Beyoncé collaborated on the theme song for Beyoncé and Cuba Gooding Jr.'s *Fighting Temptations* movie. The single wasn't a hit, but the women enjoyed working together.

Missy Elliott's mastery of the studio, her independent attitude to her career, and her songwriting talent make her the perfect role model for any aspiring musician. It almost seems an insult that her greatest hits collection had to be titled *Respect M.E.* (2007).

> **"Missy Elliott's mastery of the studio, her independent attitude to her career, and her talent for writing songs make her the perfect role model for any aspiring musician"**

Missy Elliott, as she appeared in a Gap advertisement in 2003.

A NEW DIRECTION

HONING their skills and finding their musical feet with live shows supporting K-Ci and Boyz II Men, Destiny's Child were ready to shift gears for their next album. Their record company suggested Destiny's Child consult with producer Kevin "She'kspere" Briggs. She'kspere was the boyfriend and musical partner of Kandi Burruss, a member of R & B girl group Xscape. Briggs and Burruss had just finished work with TLC, who were enjoying significant attention and global success.

Not that Mathew Knowles thought his talented girls needed the input. As Kandi recalled to *Soul Culture*: "The first time we took a trip to Texas to work with them, their manager, Beyoncé's dad, was like, 'We already know what we want to do with this album, so I don't really know what you guys are gonna bring to the table, but we'll see what you come up with.' He didn't really think we were going to come up with anything."

With *The Writing's on the Wall*, Destiny's Child took a more hands-on approach. Ten of the songs cite cowriting credits with various production and writing teams.

As a nod to their salon-practicing past, the video for the album's hottest single, "Bills, Bills, Bills," takes place in a hair salon, and the song sees the girls emerge as sassy, empowered women.

The track would spend nine weeks at the top of *Billboard*'s R & B chart, in the midst of a twenty-week residence on the Hot 100 chart. It was the longest-running R & B chart topper of 1999.

The Writing's on the Wall not only made Destiny's Child a worldwide name; it allowed Beyoncé to truly find her voice. The album was strong and innovative; what's more, the tight, clipped delivery would bring a stylistic change to the sound of contemporary R & B.

"That staccato, fast singing has kind of become the sound of R&B," Beyoncé told *The Guardian*. "We had no idea that *The Writing's on the Wall* would be as big a record as it was. Especially worldwide."

Rob Brunner, music critic at *Entertainment Weekly* magazine, praised their delivery and, like Wyclef Jean, noted the Supremes connection. He wrote: "More often they recognize the difference between extremes of pitch and extremes of passion, a distinction lost on many R&B balladeers. Destiny's Child have learned a thing or two from the Supremes, singers who knew how to use a well-placed pause or a quietly sung harmony to maximum effect."

Below: The group at the time of *The Writing's on the Wall* in 1999.

"SAY MY NAME"

WITH radio and TV lapping up the new Destiny's Child sound, the group determined to raise the stakes in their live shows. They took on a vocal coach, Kim Wood Sandusky, who helped the girls prepare for their grueling schedule, including an important tour with TLC. Sandusky remembers their incredible work ethic (on her website): "It is awesome to think back to the beginning of my work with Destiny's Child—working with them on *The Writing's on the Wall* CD. I watched the group redefine with a new look for Beyoncé, Kelly, and Michelle. We spent many hours in my vocal studio, on tour rehearsals, and in the recording studio. We had so much camaraderie on the bus as we traveled during concert tours. The one thread they all shared in common was their intense work ethic."

It is only fitting that Destiny's Child would tour with TLC in support of *The Writing's on the Wall*. At that point in time, TLC was the best-selling female group in music history. Their blockbuster album, *FanMail*, brought the trio international success with its massive singles "Unpretty" and "No Scrubs." The tour also featured a roster of incredible opening acts: K-Ci and Jojo, Christina Aguilera, Ideal, and Blaque, along with Destiny's Child.

Enjoying the taste of mainstream success, Destiny's Child released their third single, "Say My Name," in January 2000. It was cowritten and produced by Rodney "Darkchild" Jerkins and would eventually go on to become one of the group's most successful tracks.

Beyoncé particularly appreciated the input of Rodney Jerkins.

"The first time we worked with him we wrote 'Say My Name' to a track that we didn't like," she told *The Guardian*. "I don't think he liked it either. It wasn't going to make the album, and then when we were doing the photo shoot for the record my dad came into the studio and said, 'Rodney's done a new mix of that song that you hate but you just have to take a listen to it.' He played the mix to us and we couldn't even focus on anything. He had turned it into an amazing, timeless, R&B record. It was just excellent. It was one of the best songs we ever had, one of the best he's ever produced. It felt right from that moment on."

The global chart performance of "Say My Name" took the group to a new level of success, especially on a global level. In America the track debuted in the *Billboard* Hot 100 chart at number 83 and went to number one inside of three months. It also made the top spot on the *Billboard* Hot 100 Airplay chart and the *Billboard* Hot R&B/Hip-Hop Singles chart. Internationally, the song went to number one in Australia, and climbed to the number three spot in the United Kingdom. The song also gave the group their first ever number one in Asia, claiming the top slot in the Philippines for seven weeks.

A year later, at the Forty-Third Grammy Awards held on February 21, 2001, the song was awarded Best R&B Performance by a Duo or Group with Vocals and Best R&B Song—alongside nominations for Record of the Year and Song of the Year. Unfortunately, "Say My Name" would also later play a key part in the breakup of the group.

Opposite: Farrah, Kelly, Beyoncé, and Michelle performing in Las Vegas in 2000.
Following page: Beyoncé arriving at a charity event in 2000.

"I JUST HOPE PEOPLE

DON'T GET SICK OF US.

I'M SICK
OF US

AND I'M IN DESTINY'S CHILD."

"**S**AY My Name" may have been a hit, but as they were about to film the promo video for the track, LeToya Luckett and LaTavia Roberson made the shocking announcement that they no longer wanted Mathew Knowles as their manager. Talking later to MTV.com, the girls were keen to emphasize that their problems were solely with management and that they bore no ill will toward Beyoncé or Kelly Rowland. As LaTavia put it to MTV.com: "We got legal advice about it, and we got a paper written up to disaffirm our personal management contract. The paper said that we are not by any means quitting the group. We were ready, willing, and able to fulfill our duties to Destiny's Child and Columbia Records. That is a quote from the letter. It had nothing to do with Beyoncé and Kelly."

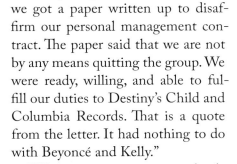

"WE WERE STRESSED AND THIS IS SUPPOSED TO BE FUN."

While never expressing clearly what their issues were with Mathew Knowles, Luckett and Roberson appear to have felt that they received less attention and were allowed less input to the group than Beyoncé and Kelly. LeToya said in the same MTV interview: "It's like 'What's going on?' We really couldn't put our finger on why we felt like that, but we just knew something was wrong with that picture, and it was a bad, almost sickening, feeling. We were stressed, and this is supposed to be fun."

With a video to shoot for "Say My Name" coming up, Mathew Knowles quickly replaced Luckett and Roberson with Monica's backing singer Michelle Williams and singer/dancer Farrah Franklin, who had appeared in the "Bills, Bills, Bills" video. Fortunately for Mathew Knowles, Michelle Williams bore a striking resemblance to LeToya, while Farrah Franklin looked a lot like LaTavia.

When the video debuted in February 2000, Luckett and Roberson were shocked to find that they had been replaced. As LaTavia told MTV.com. "So I turned on BET and they were like, 'And now the premiere of Destiny's Child's new video, 'Say My Name.'" They filed a lawsuit and later received an out-of-court monetary settlement to resolve the matter. Mathew Knowles had handled discord in the group swiftly and decisively, and far from harming the act, the publicity generated only increased media attention on a group that was about to hit the big time.

Opposite: The new line-up of Michelle Williams, Farrah Franklin, Kelly Rowland, and Beyoncé.
Following pages: The foursome performing together in 2000.

FOUR

INDEPENDENT WOMAN

INDEPENDENT WOMEN
PART 1

THE new lineup wasn't to last long. Farrah Franklin lasted five months, just long enough to feature on the group's new single, "Independent Women Part 1." Franklin had missed three shows, complained too much about Beyoncé getting the lion's share of the attention in Destiny's Child, and was seemingly unprepared for the grueling schedule the group maintained. She left the group the night before the MTV Awards, an act of unprofessionalism that Beyoncé and Rowlands could neither understand nor accept. "Destiny's Child is going to be fine," Beyoncé said in a record company statement. "We've done three or four shows already without Farrah and they've been phenomenal."

The story behind the next single, "Independent Women," was similar to that of "No No No"—with the creation of a hip remix to propel sales. Only this time, the upbeat dance version was replaced by Rodney Jerkins's slower, smoother, groove (Part 1).

The song came from a frustrated and angry Beyoncé. Lyrically, the song is tough and defiant. The Spice Girls may have been on the wane, but girl power was safe in the hands of Destiny's Child.

Mathew Knowles sent the song to Sony, their label's parent company, suggesting it might be perfect for their upcoming *Charlie's Angels* movie. Sony agreed. As Beyoncé put it to MTV.com: "I got a chance to actually write and produce the song. When the label heard it, they were like, 'The song is hot. It has to be on the *Charlie's Angels* soundtrack.' Of course, we were like, 'That would be wonderful.' So we changed it up and put a little *Charlie's Angels* flavor in it, and there it was. It was a great experience for us."

The song was released in September 2000 and took the top spot in the United Kingdom and the United States. It was a worldwide smash thanks to the power of the song and the huge popularity of the movie. The single's artwork, featuring just the three women, perfectly echoed the *Charlie's Angels* trio.

With the Spice Girls on the decline after Geri Halliwell's departure in 1998, and TLC on hiatus through 2000, the path before Destiny's Child was now clear for them to become the biggest female act in the world.

"Independent Women Part 1" reached the U.S. top spot in November 2000 and stayed there for eleven consecutive weeks, until February 2001.

Significantly for the future, the song saw the emergence of Beyoncé as writer and producer. But if *The Writing's on the Wall* was a breakthrough, then the follow-up album—*Survivor*—was the band's pinnacle.

Opposite: Kelly, Beyoncé, and Michelle at the Soul Train Lady of Soul Awards in 2000.
Above: The group making an appearance at the Texas Children's Hospital.

SURVIVOR

DESPITE the rapid success that Destiny's Child had enjoyed, Beyoncé had *not* enjoyed the media coverage regarding the personnel shifts within the group. A radio DJ joked that being in Destiny's Child was like being a contestant on the then hit TV reality show *Survivor*, on which contestants would get voted off an island weekly until there was just one left.

Beyoncé told MTV.com: "I thought about this joke that this radio station had, and they were saying, 'Oh, Destiny's Child is like *Survivor*, trying to see which member is going to last the longest on the island,' and everyone laughed. I was like, 'Ah, that's cute, but you know what? I'm going to use that negative thing and turn it into a positive thing and try to write a great song out of it.'"

Some of Beyoncé's no-holds-barred lyrics in the song that followed were interpreted by her former group colleagues LaTavia and LeToya as a thinly veiled attack. The song's line "You thought I wouldn't sell without you? Sold 9 million!" would later be quoted in a lawsuit filed by Luckett and Roberson in federal court in Houston. According to a report on *Billboard.com*, Luckett and Roberson claimed the lyrics

Above: Destiny's Child with their awards at the Grammys in 2001.
Opposite: The group performing in full Survivor mode in Sydney.

violated a previous settlement that prevented either party from making "any public comment of a disparaging nature concerning one another."

Beyoncé, however, denied that the song was a personal attack. She told *MTV*: "The song 'Survivor' is basically written for anybody that thought we weren't gonna make it. I mean, we had a deal before, with other labels, got dropped. We had a lot of people that thought that once they left us or were no longer with us anymore that we aren't gonna make it, and people automatically assume that it's about former members, and it's not. And it has that to do with it, but the song's not directed toward anybody."

Guns blazing, the song stormed up the charts. Its mission to take over the charts was foiled only by Janet Jackson's "All for You," then on a seven-week run at the top of the *Billboard* Hot 100 chart. As if to prove that Destiny's Child was truly a global act, the track entered the chart in the United Kingdom at number one in April 2001.

Significantly, the *Survivor* album saw Beyoncé flourish as writer and producer, eventually having a writing and production role on every track on the record. She told VH1: "I wrote and produced 'Independent Women Part 1' and 'Jumpin', Jumpin'.' Then I did 'Survivor' and 'Bootylicious' and the label loved it. Same with 'Nasty Girl,' 'Emotions,' 'Happy Face,' and 'Apple Pie a la Mode.' The label kept saying, 'Do another song, do another song, do another song.' It wasn't planned. It wasn't like I said, 'OK, I'm going to take charge.'"

The album received mixed reviews, with the *New York Times* unimpressed and *Entertainment Weekly* unconvinced. Rock publication *Spin*, however, took a different approach, calling the record "relentlessly inventive."

The *Survivor* album went straight to the top of the *Billboard* albums chart, selling more copies in its first week than any act in the history of Columbia Records. Globally it was a phenomenon, debuting at number one in more than nine countries and becoming the third-biggest-selling record of 2001, with almost eight million albums sold.

BOOTYLICIOUS

BEYONCÉ's musical talents flowered during the *Survivor* album sessions. She had played a significant part in the production of "Independent Women Part 1" and now stamped her musical authority on a whole album.

In a video interview with *World Pop Videos*, she explained her new role: "I produced all of the vocals and arranged all the vocals and wrote all the lyrics. I produced 'Independent Women.' I coproduced a lot before but this album—I realized we really didn't need to pay everybody all of that money when we could do it ourselves and save ourselves a couple million dollars."

The next single, "Bootylicious," deliciously mixed the R & B and rock genres together—sampling a guitar riff from Stevie Nicks's "Edge of Seventeen." Listening to the music track on an airplane, Beyoncé came up with the somewhat risqué lyrics and produced an anthem for women who weren't designed to be stick-thin magazine models. She called it an empowering song for women with some meat on their bones. More than that, it was, as she told Worldpopvideos.com, "just real funky and it makes you feel like you wanna dance." Production for the track was handled by Rob Fusari and Falonte Moore. (Fusari would be known—toward the decade's end—for his work on Lady Gaga's debut album, *The Fame*.)

The word "bootylicious" would officially enter the English lexicon—with its addition to the *Oxford English Dictionary* in 2006—defining shapely and voluptuous buttocks. Beyoncé said at the time: "I don't know what it says (officially) in the dictionary, but my definition (of bootylicious) is beautiful, bountiful, and bounce-able."

As the group members took further control of the creative process and used fewer producers, their signature sound became much clearer, with *Survivor* being their most cohesive album to date.

Survivor entered the U.S. album charts at number one in May 2001 and set a record at Columbia Records—with opening-week sales of 663,000 copies. On the back of that success, the group gave a series of high-profile performances, including Michael Jackson's Thirtieth Anniversary Celebration at Madison Square Garden in New York City (September 2001).

Unfortunately, pop music was to take a back seat to world events on September 11, 2001, when terrorists attacked the World Trade Center in New York. With flights around the world halted, the group's European tour was canceled and their U.S. dates put on hold.

In the wake of the shock and horror of 9/11, Destiny's Child would add another anthem to their list of radio hits: "Emotion"—a song originally written by brothers Barry and Robin Gibb of the Bee Gees for Australian singer Samantha Sang in 1978. The cover was a group affair, with Kelly singing the first verse, Beyoncé the second, and Michelle the third. Destiny's Child performed the powerful song, as well as a Beyoncé-arranged gospel medley, at the highly charged Concert for New York City on October 20, 2001, on a superstar bill that included David Bowie, Paul McCartney, Elton John, the Who, and Bon Jovi.

Previous pages: Destiny's Child onstage performing their massive hit "Survivor" in 2001.
Opposite: Beyoncé appearing on NBC *Today* show in 2001.
Following pages: The girls making a public appearance in New York.

"WE STARTED WHEN
WE WERE NINE YEARS OLD,
AND HERE WE ARE GETTING
A HOLLYWOOD STAR.

DREAMS
COME TRUE.

SO THANK YOU ALL SO MUCH
FOR SUPPORTING US."

CARMEN: A HIP HOPERA

NOT content with taking the reins in the recording studio for the *Survivor* album, Beyoncé now threw herself into her first acting job. The TV movie *Carmen: A Hip Hopera* came from MTV, which wanted to capitalize on the singer's global fame and undoubted screen presence. The movie was a hip-hop take on Georges Bizet's 1875 opera, with Robert Townsend (*Hollywood Shuffle*, *The Five Heartbeats*, *The Meteor Man*) being given charge of the revival as director.

Not surprisingly, the hip-hop–centered film drew more on the 1954 film *Carmen Jones*—which had been based on the 1943 Broadway musical of the same name—for inspiration than on the original opera. Beyoncé had a starring role alongside Mekhi Phifer, an up-and-coming actor who had received critical acclaim for his recent film *I Still Know What You Did Last Summer* and for television's Emmy Award–winning *A Lesson Before Dying*.

The cast featured a heavyweight lineup of music stars, including Mos Def, Rah Digga, Wyclef Jean, Da Brat, Joy Bryant, Jermaine Dupri, and Lil' Bow Wow. The music element was crucial, as director Robert Townsend explained in *Carmen: MTV's Hip Hopera—Making the Movie*: "The music is what truly makes *Carmen* unique and original because we've got some of the biggest names in rap rapping, and then we've got actors who've never rapped before."

The project was a departure for Beyoncé, but she tackled it with typical professionalism and an awareness of her own abilities. "I sang some of the songs, and I rapped some of the songs. That was another thing I was nervous about, but instead of trying to be a rapper I just talked like I would normally talk, but to the beat."

Beyoncé was more concerned about the acting side of the project, especially as she was playing an overtly sexual character. Her character, Carmen Brown, is a flirtatious, seductive waitress with aspirations to be an actress, who inadvertently causes trouble everywhere she goes. Once Carmen Brown sets her sights on an already engaged police officer, played by Mekhi Phifer, the drama quickly unfolds. Playing this brazenly sexual character was definitely a challenge to Beyoncé: "Carmen is very risqué and I wouldn't do any of the stuff that she does. I don't want anybody to think that I'm anything like Carmen Brown, 'cause I'm not!" she told *Carmen: MTV's Hip Hopera—Making the Movie*.

The film was first broadcast on May 8, 2001, exactly one week after the release of *Survivor*. Reviews were mixed, but Beyoncé came out of the project unscathed, with most critics noting her obvious potential as a movie actress.

It was more than just a new career path for Beyoncé, who had spent practically every waking moment since she was nine years old working on music. For three months she was without her family, she was apart from Kelly, and she enjoyed Hollywood. Beyoncé embraced the new experiences that California offered—from taking up yoga to trying new kinds of cuisine. As she put it to *Vibe* magazine: "Because I grew up in Houston, where the radio and culture are different, I missed out on a lot. Movies are my college. My time to go and discover."

Above: The sound track to the movie *Carmen: A Hip Hopera*.

Opposite: A glamorous Beyoncé on the red carpet at the Golden Globes in 2001.

S HORTLY after the emotionally charged Concert for New York City on October 20, 2001, Destiny's Child released a Christmas album that they had been working on over the summer. With European tour dates canceled and American tour dates postponed, they were able to devote their time and energy to promoting the album. The record featured traditional Christmas tunes like "Do You Hear What I Hear?" and "Silent Night," as well as four original numbers.

The album closed with what would be the group's third dedication to Andretta Tillman—a gospel medley of "Holy Is the Lamb," "Jesus Loves Me," and "Total Praise." This final tribute to Andretta was followed by a spiritual toast to the future, "Outro (DC-3) Thank You," which gives thanks to God for the blessing of Michelle's addition to the group.

In 2001, there was no greater marketing vehicle in America than Oprah Winfrey's daytime talk show, *Oprah*. Destiny's Child performed the new song "8 Days of Christmas"—written by Beyoncé and Errol "Poppi" McCalla Jr.—on the show. The appearance on *Oprah* boosted sales, the album sold remarkably well for a Christmas album (they rarely perform as well as regular releases), and it climbed to number 34 on the U.S. album chart.

Billboard's Artists of the Year had, despite a few trials and tribulations, finished on a high note. Destiny's Child even got to appear on *Sesame Street*, singing "A New Way to Walk" with Elmo and Grover.

If the Christmas album revealed the more mellow side of Destiny's Child, then the next release—*This Is the Remix*—was a timely reminder of their place in contemporary urban music. The album was a twelve-track remix featuring past contributions from Wyclef Jean, Missy Elliott, Static Major, Da Brat, Jermaine Dupri, and Lil' Bow Wow. Beyoncé, Kelly, and Michelle redid some of the vocals, even including "Dot (The E-Poppi Mix)," a song that had previously only been released on the sound track to the *Charlie's Angels* movie.

Sadly, the release of the remix album brought back some of the emnity brought about by the departure of Luckett and Roberson, in particular with the reappearance of "Survivor." Once again, a lawsuit was filed regarding the breach—exhibited on the extended remix of "Survivor"—of their previous agreement barring each party from public disparagement. The song's win at the forty-third Grammy Awards in February 2001, a month prior to that, for Best R&B Performance by a Duo or Group with Vocals, only increased the tension.

But if the personnel disputes were from the past, then one track was a very clear indicator of Destiny's Child's future. "Heard a Word" featured just Michelle Williams; it was a song from her upcoming solo album, *Heart to Yours*. It seemed that all the girls were thinking about a life outside Destiny's Child.

Following tours in Japan and Europe during May and June of 2002, the group resolved that a break was needed. It had been a tough twelve-month period, and with Luckett and Roberson's lawsuit finally resolved, the group announced that they would start working on some solo projects before working together and recording any new material as Destiny's Child.

Opposite: The women pose with their own dolls at the Toys "R" Us store in New York, 2001.

"THERE'S DEFINITELY A

DANGEROUS
FEELING

WHEN YOU'RE IN LOVE.

IT'S GIVING YOUR HEART

TO SOMEONE ELSE AND

KNOWING THAT THEY

HAVE CONTROL OVER

YOUR FEELINGS."

GOLDMEMBER

COMIC actor and writer Mike Myers was two movies into his Austin Powers British spy spoof series when he approached Beyoncé to appear in the third installment in the series, *Austin Powers in Goldmember*. The movie introduced Michael Caine as Austin's father, Nigel Powers, and featured a host of cameo appearances by A-list stars—from Tom Cruise and Gwyneth Paltrow to Steven Spielberg, John Travolta, and the Osbournes.

Despite having done relatively well in her first acting role, in *Carmen: A Hip Hopera*, Beyoncé was nervous about tackling a big-screen movie. She told the BBC: "I was very nervous, I didn't really know what I was doing. I was just grateful to get the opportunity. I didn't really think what would happen if it did go bad—I just did it and tried to do the best I could. I tried to learn—I felt like it was a new chapter of my life. A new way to grow as an artist."

But with Mike Myers setting the movie in the 1970s, Beyoncé was attracted to

Below: Enjoying a comedy moment with Mike Myers as Austin Powers in *Goldmember*.

the project and was happy to meet the comedian and audition for him. Speaking of the movie and of her interest in the seventies, she told *The Scottish Daily Record*: "The style, the fashion, the music, and the whole attitude—they held their own bodies very strong. It was all about soul, you know. I loved it. I loved the hair, I've always loved Aretha Franklin. . . . Then I got a call from Mike Myers who said he really wanted me to play this character from the seventies who had this hair, wore these clothes, and had this attitude. It was almost like 'Oh my God, this is perfect,' and that's how it all worked out."

Once Beyoncé put on the seventies-style outfit, complete with Afro wig, and read through some scenes with Mike Myers, the producers knew she could handle the part. "She just came in and nailed it," producer John Lyons told *Ebony* magazine.

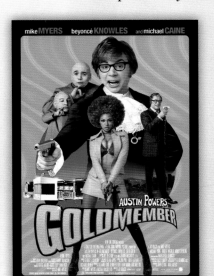

Beyoncé's character was loosely inspired by Pam Grier's sassy character Foxy Brown in the 1970s blaxploitation movie of the same name. As Beyoncé put it to *Film Monthly* when discussing her character, Foxy Cleopatra "kicks people's butts and she is very funny, with a dry sense of humor."

Beyoncé first appears in a nightclub scene, singing "Hey, Goldmember" as part of a trio featuring her younger sister, Solange, and the singer Devin. The film earned great reviews and was a box office smash, grossing over $270 million. If she had decided to pursue an acting career, Beyoncé was set. The film also kept her musical career bubbling by playing her first-ever solo single over the closing credits. The song, "Work It Out," was produced by ace production duo the Neptunes (Pharrell Williams and Chad Hugo), who would be named top producers of the 2000s by *Billboard*.

Goldmember dramatically raised Beyoncé's public profile and helped her emerge as a solo artist. Naturally, with entrepreneur Mathew Knowles still steering the ship, promotional opportunities blossomed and Beyoncé proved to be the perfect pitchwoman.

Adweek national news editor Jack Feuer explained Beyoncé's appeal to *Billboard*: "She's the entrance to the dance. She has glamor, a youthful exuberance, and a love of life."

The film also opened doors for the star outside the music industry as she became known worldwide in her own right outside of Destiny's Child. Her power to endorse and sell products was recognized. Beyoncé started out small with her endorsements—some of the first companies she worked with were Houston-based Pro-Line hair products and Candie's shoes in New York. Then in 2002 she was asked to represent Pepsi in place of Britney Spears. This was a big deal. Other stars of Pepsi commercials have included high-profile celebrities such as Michael Jackson, Shakira, and Cindy Crawford. Pepsi told the press, "Beyoncé Knowles, the lead singer of the multi-platinum selling trio Destiny's Child and big-screen star of *Austin Powers in Goldmember*, has joined the Pepsi family." Beyoncé, in return, was delighted, stating, "I've been a fan of Pepsi's TV ads for as long as I can remember. I'm thrilled to be joining so many talented entertainers who have created memorable Pepsi moments over the years. Many of them have inspired me, and I'd love to do the same for the next generation of artists out there."

Above: Beyoncé in promotional posters for *Goldmember*.

Pages 82–83: Beyoncé on the Jay Leno show in 2003.

JANET JACKSON

Being the youngest child in a legendary soul music dynasty didn't make things easy for Janet Jackson. Just as with her elder siblings, she was groomed from an early age by their domineering father, Joe, to be a singer and performer. Her father signed her to a record deal when she was sixteen, and *Janet Jackson* (1982) sounds dated and dull. Despite that, and on the back of her starring in the popular TV show *Diff'rent Strokes*, it sold well, making number six on the *Billboard* chart.

Her sophomore release, *Dream Street* (1984) was less successful, despite the presence of elder brother Marlon and Giorgio Moroder as producers. At the age of eighteen Janet showed her independent spirit when she eloped with a member of a different singing family, James DeBarge (the marriage lasted less than a year). She also refused to have her father involved in the recording of her third album, and because of that, *Control* (1986) turned out to be a fantastic musical statement of independence. Single releases, including the title track, "Nasty," and "What Have You Done for Me Lately," were enormous international hits, all propelled by producers Jimmy Jam and Terry Lewis's trademark big snare and electronic bass sound. The uniform design of her and her dancers' costumes suggested a militaristic resistance to all attempts at control over Janet. Her vibrant, brilliantly choreographed live performances set standards for performance of live gigs that other stars struggled to match.

Control made Janet one of the biggest female stars in the business, and she capitalized on the success with the release of her socially responsible *Janet Jackson's Rhythm Nation 1814* in 1989. It was as successful as its predecessor, but instead of following it up with another album release, Jackson took time out to make her movie debut, in *Poetic Justice* (1993), with Tupac Shakur, directed by John Singleton. Jackson plays the part of a ghetto poet, Justice, in a romantic movie set among harsh scenes of domesticity.

Her refusal to follow standard music business rules has made for an interesting career. She has made mistakes along the way, including an infamous "wardrobe malfunction" during her Super Bowl performance of 2004, and moves into "difficult" territory with albums like *The Velvet Rope* (1997) with its S and M theme and *Discipline* (2008) with its teen-lust focus have not made her life easy. Neither have her public spats with siblings and parents, and her very public support of brother Michael when he was accused of child molestation. Yet her willingness to address matters head-on, to confront and question people who would control her, have offered inspiration for any female artist striving to make it in show business in the twenty-first century.

> **"Her willingness to address matters head-on, to confront and question people who would control her, have offered inspiration for any female artist striving to make it in show business in the twenty-first century."**

Opposite: Janet Jackson's independent spirit and onstage style have influenced Beyoncé.

SUPERSTAR LOVE MATCH

I N October 2001, at the Concert for New York City, Beyoncé met record label boss and rap superstar Jay-Z for the first time. It was the beginning of a relationship that would significantly shape Beyoncé's artistic and personal future.

By the time Beyoncé met Jay-Z, whose real name is Shawn Corey Carter, the rapper was already a major figure in the music world. He had his own record label and clothing line and was poised to become one of the most successful and influential music executives in the world.

Like Beyoncé, Shawn Carter grew up loving music, especially his childhood favorite, Michael Jackson. But while Beyoncé's childhood was spent in a safe middle-class suburb of Houston, Carter was raised in one of the most dangerous neighborhoods in America, the Marcy Projects in Brooklyn.

He witnessed shootings, his first at just nine years of age, and was shot at several times over the years. He told Andrew Marr of the BBC: "We had great days and played outside, normal childhood, but some days, when it got bad, people were shooting at twelve noon on Sundays."

The extremely addictive street drug, crack, was a major issue. Jay-Z told the CBS television program *60 Minutes* that the cocaine-based drug had taken hold in his community. "It was a plague in that neighborhood," he explained: "It was just everywhere, everywhere you looked . . . you could smell it in the hallways."

Fortunately, music was a way out, as Jay-Z explained to Andrew Marr: "My mother and father, before they separated, they had the biggest record collection in the neighborhood. Everyone came to our house to listen to music and have fun."

With a gift for wordplay, Carter became the best rapper in his neighborhood. Though he was unable to secure a record deal, his business savvy kicked in at a young age. Carter and his friends Damon Dash and Kareem Biggs started their own label—Roc-A-Fella Records—and sold CDs from the trunk of a car.

Jay-Z and Beyoncé found common ground in music, and a shared understanding that hard work is the bedrock for any career in the entertainment business. Jay-Z's childhood poverty stayed with him as he accumulated millions of dollars. "Being broke is a great motivator," he told British talk show host Jonathan Ross. Beyoncé may not have had the same financial hardships to overcome, but she too was driven to devote everything she had to her career.

From the beginning of her relationship with Jay-Z, Beyoncé, now pretty media savvy, decided to keep her private life as private as possible. In a 2003 interview with *Glamour* magazine, she stated, "I've learned that it's better if I don't talk about my personal life relationships." The well-guarded romance between the controversial rapper who had stabbed another record executive and the squeaky-clean girl group singer would fascinate and intrigue the world's media for the rest of the decade.

What Jay-Z and Beyoncé didn't hide, however, was their musical partnership, which began with Beyoncé adding vocals to "03 Bonnie & Clyde," the lead single for Jay-Z's seventh studio album, *The Blueprint 2: The Gift & The Curse*. While Beyoncé took a break from Destiny's Child, she allowed herself to absorb the music world Jay-Z moved in.

Opposite: Jay-Z and Beyoncé performing together at the 2003 MTV Video Music Awards.
Following pages: The couple at the 2011 U.S. Open Tennis Championship.

FIVE

ME, MYSELF, AND I

A STARRING ROLE

WITH Destiny's Child on hold, Beyoncé was free to pursue other ambitions. *The Fighting Temptations,* her next film project, was an upbeat moral tale crammed with inspirational music. Beyoncé played the part of Lily, a single mother who sings non-church music in a local bar. Consequently she's shunned by the righteous members of the local Church of Beulah. When Lily's childhood friend Darren, played by Cuba Gooding Jr., returns to Georgia for his aunt's funeral he discovers he has an inheritance, with strings attached. His $150,000 depends on him taking the church choir to a state singing contest. Which is where Beyoncé comes in, since the choir is terrible. Beyoncé explained the premise to Wayne Brady on his TV show: "Darren, who is Cuba Gooding Jr., is from New York and he's this big city slickster and he goes back to a small town to get his inheritance and in order to get his money he has to lead this choir to success. He sees me in a nightclub and he asks me to be a part of it and I join the choir and it takes them a while to accept me. The music is incredible. The message is incredible. You want to take your parents to see it, your kids to see it."

Beyoncé clearly felt comfortable with the movie being set around a church. It made her "feel at home," she told the CBS morning news program *The Early Show,* and explained that the movie is about "coming home and finding what's important to you."

With typical professionalism she prepared herself for the leading role by taking acting lessons, telling iVillage.com, "I've been working with someone and it's going good. I've learned so much about myself. I've learned you have to pull from things and think about things that I never really thought about. I'm sure it's definitely going to also inspire me to write different songs and different types of music."

Music also played an important role with legendary soul and gospel acts in the cast including The O'Jays (as the singing barbers who help out the choir), Shirley Caesar, Faith Evans, and Melba Moore. Beyoncé reveled in working with some of her heroes. As she told entertainment reporter Jimmy Carter, "Gospel has had such an influence on all different kinds of music, so for me to be around these people was incredible," she said. "When we sang together it didn't feel like we were doing a movie." The movie's soundtrack album was pretty impressive. Beyoncé recorded tracks with artists P. Diddy, Missy Elliott, and Destiny's Child and three solo tracks, "Swing Low, Sweet Chariot," "Fever," and "He Still Loves Me."

When asked to reveal her acting inspirations Beyoncé said, "I would have to say Barbra Streisand and Diana Ross in *Mahogany* and all the other movies. They were singers and they were successful and did not have to act, financially or for any other reasons, but they did because they wanted to and they loved it and were talented and gifted at it. I don't think there's anything wrong with combining music and film . . . But I do want to eventually do a movie where I'm not a singer."

Opposite: Budding movie star Beyoncé at the premiere of *The Fighting Temptations.*
Above: The singer in a scene from the film with costar Cuba Gooding Jr.

91

ME, MYSELF, AND I

CRAZY IN LOVE

THE rumor mill regarding Destiny's Child's future kicked into high gear once the girls began to release solo projects. The first solo album to appear was *Heart to Yours* by Michelle Williams; it was released on April 16, 2002, and became the best-selling gospel album of the year. Next came Kelly Rowland's debut *Simply Deep*, in October of that same year, which included the worldwide hit "Dilemma," with rapper Nelly.

As Beyoncé put the finishing touches on her release, she spoke often about the need of each member to find her own voice. She was delighted at the success of Kelly and Michelle, as she told Dennis Hensley of *Glamour* magazine in 2003: "I was really proud when Kelly got nominated for the Grammy with Nelly for 'Dilemma.' And with Michelle, I saw her performing on a TV show and you could just see that she was at peace and happy with herself." Beyoncé continually talked about the new Destiny's Child album that was on the table later in the year. Although for now she was promoting "Crazy in Love" from her upcoming debut solo album, Destiny's Child remained intact and was not about to break apart.

With the singer's first solo single, "Work It Out," officially under her belt (from the *Austin Powers in Goldmember* sound track), Beyoncé felt confident about her forthcoming single, "Crazy in Love," to be released in May 2003.

She told *Glamour* magazine: "The song talks about how, when you're falling in love, you do things that are out of character and you don't really care because you're just open. The song came from me actually looking crazy one day in the studio. I said, 'I'm lookin' crazy right now,' and Rich Harrison, the producer, was like, 'That's the song!'"

Rich Harrison had made waves the previous year as the writer and producer of Amerie's gold-selling debut album, *All I Have*. Sampling the horn section from "Are You My Woman (Tell Me So)"—a 1970 song by the Chi-Lites—"Crazy in Love" would appeal to listeners of all ages with its infectious mix of funk and soul. When Jay-Z added a rap in the studio late one night, the song was complete. "Crazy in Love" was an immediate smash, staying at number one in the United States for eight weeks and topping the singles charts in the United Kingdom, Australia, Canada, Denmark, Ireland, Italy, New Zealand, the Netherlands, Norway, Sweden, and Switzerland. The song, and its accompanying video, which saw Beyoncé introduce her trademark booty dance, perfectly prepared the ground for the upcoming album. Critics were on board, too, with the esteemed Anthony DeCurtis of *Rolling Stone* saying, "'Crazy in Love' . . . roars out of the speakers on the strength of a propulsive horn sample and the charged presence of her pal, Jay-Z."

The record industry appreciated Beyoncé's first single too. Beyoncé won two Grammy awards for the song in 2004, picking up Best R&B Song and Best Rap/Sung Collaboration. She won again at the BET Awards, and remarkably, "Crazy in Love" also won the Single of the Year Award from the rock-oriented *New Musical Express* in England, after the magazine's review called Beyoncé's debut single "a 100 per cent, stone-cold, dead-cert, classic."

Previous pages: A radiant Beyoncé and dancers performing at the Jingle Bell Ball in New York in 2003.
Opposite: A solo Beyoncé at the 2003 Essence Awards show.

THE world got a taster of Beyoncé's first solo album with the worldwide hit "Crazy in Love" and *Dangerously in Love* did not disappoint. She introduced the album on a Pepsi Smash promo interview, saying, "The solo album experience has been a big step for me as far as [*sic*] artist, entertainer, a songwriter, a woman. It's something I'd been anticipating a long time and I had so many ideas I wanted to express. Everyone's so excited about the single and I'm very anxious for people to hear it. It's my baby."

Rather than spending a few weeks on the project, as she had with Destiny's Child albums, Beyoncé took her time with what she knew would be a vital first album. By this time, she'd grown up rapidly, met movie stars, experienced Hollywood, and was discovering a new music scene through Jay-Z. His influence and Beyoncé's growing maturity into both a woman and a solo artist would become evident on *Dangerously in Love*.

The album's fifteen songs were whittled down from more than forty that had been recorded in several locations across America by Beyoncé and her team of producers. Despite this committee approach, once more Beyoncé managed to record an album with a strong, cohesive identity. The record delightfully mixes hip-hop, rock, and jazz, and her choice of guest artists covers all the pop music bases, from Missy Elliott to Luther Vandross, Big Boi from OutKast, and of course, her beau, Jay-Z.

"WHEN I'M CREATING, I JUST DO WHATEVER'S IN MY HEART."

Beyoncé wanted to make a more mature more personal, album. She discussed the tone of the new material with *Glamour* magazine: "Some are really sexy, more sexy than anything I've done before. And some are just so honest and personal, like the song about my father, 'Daddy.' For some songs, I didn't even write anything down, I just spoke from my heart. When I'm creating, I just do whatever's in my heart—then after I finish, I'm like, 'Oh, okay, I have to let people hear this!'"

Beyoncé managed to draw on various musical styles for this record, somehow weaving it all into a Beyoncé sound. "Hip Hop Star" is a screaming, guitar-heavy mix of funk and hip-hop, while "Be with You" is pure melodic R & B. Jay-Z raps as only Jay-Z can on "Jumpin' Jumpin'," but that track sits easily alongside the breezy trip-hop of "Yes." The duet with Luther Vandross, "The Closer I Get," is a spirited nod to her musical roots, while the snapping guitar on it perfectly matches the tough, independent, voice of Beyoncé's accomplished lyrics.

Talking about one of her favorite tracks, "Me, Myself and I," on a record company *Making of Dangerously in Love* promo video, Beyoncé expressed the kind of

self-awareness and maturity that suggested the new album would deliver on all her talent and promise.

She explained: "'Me, Myself and I' was a great song for women. Relationships are not always smooth . . . most women look back and they are thinking, 'God, I'm smarter than that! All that BS. I should have known better.' But the way I look at it, you take that experience and think of it as a growing experience. You always have yourself, and you can always depend on yourself. It's basically a celebration of a break-up."

Above: The star performing at the 2003 MTV Europe Music Awards.

IN August 2003, Beyoncé stepped out of Destiny's Child's shadow and performed at the annual MTV Music Awards alongside Jay-Z. She was lowered from the rafters of Radio City Music Hall in New York City, upside down, before landing in a chair while singing "Baby Boy." She then switched to "Crazy in Love," complete with booty dance and Jay-Z's highly charged rap. The star picked up a few awards too, winning Best R&B Video, Best Female Video, and Best Choreography for "Crazy in Love."

Before offering her new solo show to American audiences, Beyoncé headed for Europe on the *Dangerously in Love* tour at the tail end of 2003. A live DVD was recorded over two nights that November, at Wembley in London. Fans were delighted at the scale of the spectacle combined with powerfully emotional musical performances from the ever-improving Beyoncé, who performed alongside her troupe of dancers in front of a large video backdrop.

Although material from *Dangerously in Love* dominated the performance, Beyoncé also dedicated a segment in the show to Destiny's Child back catalog with

"Bug a Boo," "No No No (Part 2)," "Bootylicious," and "Jumpin', Jumpin'"), as well as drawing on songs from the *Fighting Temptations* sound track.

Melissa Tang reviewed the concert for www.the-situation. co.uk: "As the stage cleared and the lights dimmed, there seemed to be only one song that the sexy star had not yet performed— her British number one 'Crazy in Love.' The crowd jumped to their feet as soon as they heard the unmistakable beat, and sure enough, Miss Knowles appeared in a glittering silver dress, launching into her debut solo single. The sound of the whole arena singing along with her, word for word, was astounding, and the beaming smile on Beyoncé's face said it all. When two male dancers stripped off their overcoat and hat, the girls in the audience went mad, and the screams became deafening as the one and only Jay-Z ran on stage to spit his verse halfway through the track."

It was a remarkable and triumphant finish to a year that unambiguously validated her decision to go solo. Beyoncé's first solo album had made it to number one, and her two singles that year, "Crazy in Love" and "Baby Boy," spent seventeen weeks on the top spot between them.

Just before the UK tour in November, Beyoncé and her manager-father Mathew were involved in some high-finance deals that would astound the music business. British-based music company Sanctuary paid £6.6 million for Mathew Knowles's management company Music World Entertainment. It was a surprising purchase for Sanctuary, which had historically been a rock music company focusing on bands like Iron Maiden and Guns N' Roses. Mathew Knowles agreed to stay on at Sanctuary and build an urban and gospel division, developing new artists. The deal lasted just a couple of years. On March 10, 2006, it was announced that the ownership of Music World Entertainment and the Music World Music Record Label would revert once again to Beyoncé's father.

Previous pages: Beyoncé and Stevie Wonder performing at the VH1 Divas Duets concert in 2003.
Opposite: Deccending to the stage at London's Wembley arena and (above) as cover girl of *Honey* magazine.

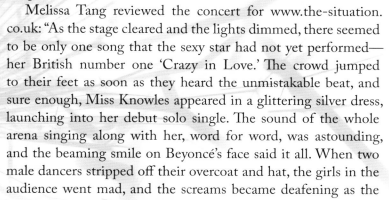

A MERICA'S most-watched sporting event, the Super Bowl came to the Reliant Stadium in Houston on February 1, 2004. The New England Patriots would play against the Carolina Panthers, and Beyoncé, a local girl made good, was asked to sing the national anthem to begin the proceedings.

As Beyoncé was escorted to the stage by General Peter Pace, she cut a sophisticated, elegant figure dressed in a no-frills white suit. The outfit may have been understated, but her powerful delivery of "The Star-Spangled Banner" was simply spectacular. She sang the American national anthem with a staggering display of technique, emotion, and personal style. It was one of the finest renditions of the American national anthem seen at a Super Bowl. Once again, Beyoncé had taken on a challenge and nailed it.

Unfortunately, Beyoncé's performance, and indeed the game itself—the New England Patriots defeated the Carolina Panthers in what *Sports Illustrated* writer Peter King hailed as the "greatest Super Bowl of all time"—was overshadowed by Janet Jackson's notorious wardrobe malfunction (exposing a breast on live TV), broadcast during the all-star half-time show.

With *Dangerously in Love* making such an impact on radio and TV in 2003, it was likely that Beyoncé would fare well at the 2004 Grammy Awards, held in New York on February 8. Much to her delight she was invited to open the show with one of her childhood idols, Prince. It was a rare outing for Prince, and Beyoncé was apprehensive and nervous about working with one of her idols.

She told Giantlife.com: "I was terrified, walking into rehearsals I was so overwhelmed and nervous and star-struck. We rehearsed every day for an hour for a week. It was Prince's idea as he knows people are star-struck, and it made me really comfortable. And by the time it came to do it [*sic*], it was second nature."

Beyoncé and Prince performed a medley of Prince's hits, including "Purple Rain," "Baby, I'm a Star," and "Let's Go Crazy," as well Beyoncé's "Crazy in Love."

Beyoncé was barely containable onstage. Her enthusiasm at being on stage with Prince was clear for everyone to see. In retrospect, she felt she might have overdone her performance, allowing her Sasha Fierce alter ego—the character she used to turn the shy Houston church girl into a world-famous diva—to take over. When she watched a tape of her performance sometime later, she was shocked at her own performance. Contactmusic.com quoted Beyoncé as saying, "I saw that I didn't even give him [Prince] the mic. It was supposed to be in the middle, not in front of my mouth. Sasha just took over."

Beyoncé performed again later in the show, singing "Dangerously in Love." She won a record-breaking five Grammys that night, including Best Female R&B Vocal Performance and Best Contemporary R&B Album (for *Dangerously in Love*), while her duet with Luther Vandross won Best R&B Performance by a Duo or Group with Vocals. Accepting the award from Gwen Stefani and Quentin Tarantino, Beyoncé said: "I want to thank the Grammys for giving me this opportunity. This was my first record as a solo artist and I want to thank everyone involved, Scott Torch, Rich Harrison, and Jay-Z, Angela Beyincé, Fanatic. I wanna thank Columbia. I want to thank my parents. This is unbelievable, Kelly and Michelle. . . ."

Opposite: An exuberant Beyoncé onstage with Prince at the Grammys.

"I AM A WORKAHOLIC AND I DON'T BELIEVE IN NO. I DON'T BELIEVE IN I NEED TO SLEEP. IF I'M NOT SLEEPING NOBODY'S SLEEPING. I'M ONE HUMAN BEING. IT'S A LOT."

DESTINY FULFILLED

O N March 12, 2004, Beyoncé took on her first major tour as a solo artist as co-headliner of the Verizon Ladies First Tour. Tagged "the urban Lilith Fair," the triple-headliner event featured Beyoncé, Alicia Keys, and Missy Elliott, alongside Canadian singer Tamia, who opened as a special guest.

Covering thirty dates, the Verizon tour promoted recent albums by the women—*This Is Not a Test!* by Missy Elliott, *The Diary of Alicia Keys* by Alicia Keys, *More* by Tamia, and Beyoncé's *Dangerously in Love*. It was the first major tour to highlight women in the "urban" (hip-hop and R & B) scene. Expressing a fondness for this rare display of sisterhood, Beyoncé told *USA Today*, "Even before I started putting my album together last year, I wanted to get together a tour with other women. I know that you have a lot of types of tours with other types of artists, but not just strictly hip hop and R&B women."

Elliott was a longtime Destiny's Child and Beyoncé collaborator, but few knew about Beyoncé's history with Alicia Keys. Keys elaborated on their relationship to *USA Today*: "What a lot of people don't realize is that I've known Beyoncé since we were both at Columbia Records and we used to do showcases together."

Beyoncé not only enjoyed the camaraderie of the tour; she visibly blossomed as a performer. *Entertainment Weekly* was at the Fort Lauderdale concert, reporting: "Through blinding costume changes, lascivious choreography, deafeningly reverbed melisma, and glorified invocations of everyone retro—from James Brown to Tina Turner to, well, Destiny's Child—Beyoncé connected directly with 'us,' thanks to her winning smile."

The closing of the Verizon tour saw Beyoncé back in the studio—with Kelly Rowland and Michelle Williams—for the group's fourth album. Beyoncé told MTV that the album was a perfect way to end on a high note.

"It's not our last record because one of us wants to go solo, or because we don't get along, or because we don't like each other anymore, or because of cattiness," Knowles said. "It's because it's the end of this chapter in our lives. We've been doing this for fourteen years now, and our destinies have been fulfilled."

The record presented the three blossoming artists equally and, overall, it was tougher and more urban than the pop-heavy albums of the past. Destiny's Child started a world tour in April 2005. They traveled through Australia, Japan, and Dubai, then on through Europe before kicking off the U.S. leg that summer in New Orleans. It was a greatest hits affair, covering all their best musical moments. Tickets sold fast and reviewers were impressed, but time was running out to see the group performing together.

On June 11, 2005, in Barcelona, Spain, Kelly Rowland announced on stage that that night's show was to be the final performance for Destiny's Child. A subsequent statement to MTV was assured the fans that relations were good between the girls. Destiny's Child had fulfilled their destiny, was the simple message, "No matter what happens, we will always love each other as friends and sisters and will always support each other as artists. We want to thank all of our fans for their incredible love and support and hope to see you all again as we continue fulfilling our destinies."

Previous pages: Beyoncé onstage at WGCI's Big Jam V in Chicago.
Opposite: Destiny's Child together again in 2004.

THE PINK PANTHER

HAVING performed admirably opposite comedian Mike Myers in *Austin Powers in Goldmember* and with Cuba Good Jr. in *The Fighting Temptations*, Beyoncé's next big-screen adventure was in a revival of the Pink Panther franchise. Comedy great Steve Martin took on the role of bumbling Inspector Clouseau, a role that had been originally played in a series of popular films by British actor Peter Sellers in the 1960s and 1970s. Other high profile actors in the film included Kevin Kline, Jean Reno, and Emily Mortimer.

Beyoncé was approached for the movie by director Shawn Levy. Levy, who had had a hit—*Cheaper by the Dozen*—with Steve Martin had also worked with Beyoncé many years previously for a Disney sitcom pilot. Beyoncé told IGN.com, "It was my first acting gig and I hope nobody ever finds it. Jett Jackson. He remembered working with me and I remember he said, 'You're gonna be an actor one day. I'm gonna remember you.' And he called and told me about Xania . . . that she was an international superstar and singer . . . At first I thought, 'I don't want to play another part like that, because I don't have time to do the research.' [long pause] Then he told me Kevin Kline and Steve Martin were gonna be a part of it and I said, 'I gotta do it.'"

Knowles, always aiming at being a triple threat, watched Steve Martin as writer and actor closely. As she told IGN.com, "The biggest thing was probably from watching Steve Martin, because he is so professional and so serious and he's been doing it for a long time and you can just see that in his mannerisms. When he's in-between his takes, he goes from being this wacky, unbelievable character, to becoming Steve Martin and working with the director and changing things and writing the script. I'm a songwriter and a performer, so I respect that and hopefully one day I'll do that…"

Filmed on location in New York and Paris, *The Pink Panther* was a lightweight comedy, filled with slapstick and bawdy humor. Beyoncé played the role of world-famous pop star Xania, the girlfriend of the man who owns the Pink Panther diamond. Xania becomes involved with Inspector Clouseau (Steve Martin) when her boyfriend is found dead. Clouseau falls for Xania's flirtatious charms, and a series of mishaps ensue.

Once again, Beyoncé was at pains to assure interviewers that she was nothing like her sexually manipulative character, telling IGN.com: "I'm kind of like that onstage. I'm very much so like that onstage. But I'm not like that in real life. It's a character, so it's a part of the acting."

Beyoncé also contributed two songs to the movie, "A Woman Like Me" and "Check on It."

The movie received mixed reviews, with Hollywood trade bible *Variety* calling it "neither the disaster one might have suspected nor a fully realized madcap farce." Ultimately the movie was another box office smash for Beyoncé, with the film taking the number one spot on its release and quickly becoming the highest-grossing film in the Pink Panther series.

Opposite: Beyoncé filming *The Pink Panther* on the streets of New York.
Above: The star as Xania in a promotional poster for the film.

B'DAY

BEYONCÉ's follow-up album to *Dangerously in Love* had originally been planned for release in early 2004, but she delayed production to work on the *Destiny Fulfilled* album and tour. When she was offered the role of Deena in the *Dreamgirls* movie, Beyoncé once again delayed her album. It was eventually released on September 4, 2006—Beyoncé's twenty-fifth birthday, which, of course, explains the album's title *B'Day*.

Once again Beyoncé arranged, wrote, and produced all the tracks on the album, aided by a team of the hottest producers around, notably Sean Garrett, Rich Harrison, Rodney Jerkins, the Neptunes, and Swizz Beatz.

The album was produced over an intense three-week period at the Sony Music Studios in New York. Beyoncé rented out all the studios in the building and worked simultaneously on tracks, moving from one producer to another, listening, making suggestions, and honing the songs that would eventually make it onto the finished record.

Young songwriter Makeba Riddick, who was brought in by Beyoncé for the *B'day* album, was amazed at the singer's work ethic. She told MTV: "We worked together every day, pulling 14-hour days. I see the reason why she is the biggest artist of our generation: Her work ethic is unlike anything I've ever seen. She would tell us to be there at 11 o'clock in the morning and we would be there until, like, four or five in the morning. But she would be there before 11 a.m. When we got there, she was already there, working."

The album reveled in a mix of new sounds for Beyoncé—hard beats, seventies-style funk, and driving guitar—all meshed in a seductive multilayered production, given extra force by the use of live instruments in the studio. As a singer Beyoncé delivered her most intense, powerful vocals to date. Thematically the material veered between tender love songs and her now trademark battles of the sexes.

The album entered the U.S. *Billboard* Hot 200 chart at number one, selling a cool 541,000 copies in the first week alone. It was the album's third single that really took off. "Irreplaceable" became America's top-selling single of 2007.

Beyoncé held open auditions for an all-female band that she named Suga Mama to tour the album.

She told MTV.com: "I wanted to get together a group of fierce, talented, hungry, beautiful women and form an all-girl band . . . I'm all about female empowerment."

On April 10, 2007, Knowles embarked on the Beyoncé Experience Tour. The tour started in Tokyo, taking on shows around the world. It visited more than ninety venues worldwide and was later made into the concert DVD *The Beyoncé Experience Live!* The show was an up-tempo, two-hour affair with Beyoncé leading from the front, never letting the pace drop—constantly pushing the band to give 100 percent and match her own staggeringly high-energy performance. With more than thirty songs and some six costume changes, Beyoncé had raised the bar for live performance, winning glowing reviews around the world. The *London Evening Standard*'s John Aizlewood described it perfectly: "Big, brave, and bold, the Beyoncé Experience is how pop music would work if it were choreographed by Busby Berkeley."

ME, MYSELF, AND I

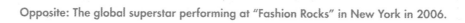

"I GET NERVOUS WHEN
I DON'T GET NERVOUS. IF I'M

NERVOUS

I KNOW I'M GOING TO HAVE

A GOOD SHOW."

DREAMGIRLS

T H E movie version of the successful *Dreamgirls* Broadway show opened on Christmas Day 2006. It's the story of a fictional female singing trio, the Dreams, and their search for success in the 1960s.

Jamie Foxx, fresh from his Oscar-winning performance as Ray Charles in the movie *Ray*, plays tough-talking manager Curtis Taylor Jr. Eddie Murphy plays James "Thunder" Early, a down-on-his-luck soul music legend, while Beyoncé is Deena Jones, a Diana Ross–like singer whom Jamie Foxx discovers singing in a trio.

Initially, the girls sing backup for James "Thunder" Early. But when they branch out on their own, Beyoncé's character is picked as the lead singer, a move that causes bad feeling within the group, since Effie (played by *American Idol*'s Jennifer Hudson) is clearly a far better singer. And so the drama begins.

Beyoncé wanted to focus one hundred percent on a movie role that was very important to her. She'd been a fan of the show since she was a teenager. "Oh God, I just light up when I talk [about that movie] because I wanted it so bad," she told MTV. She had screen tests in New York during the Destiny's Child farewell

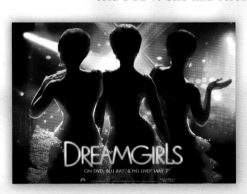

tour and studied the Michael Bennett choreography for the stage show and had the moves down perfectly by the time she met with director Bill Condon. Although the movie used new choreography, the director was impressed with the Houston singer's dedication and commitment to get the role.

She told *MTV.com*: "I really had to prove myself, but after they saw it, they were like, 'OK, she is Deena.'"

It was surprising that Beyoncé wasn't cast as Effie—the powerhouse singer who ends up destitute—but Beyoncé was just happy to be in the movie. She told *Blackfilm.com*, "I didn't care that Deena was not the star in the script. I just wanted to be a part of the film and a part of something that's so relevant and so exciting and I think history. I think twenty years from now people will still be watching the film."

Determined to prove herself as an actress, Beyoncé also took acting classes with teacher Ivana Chuban, telling *Blackfilm.com*, "I told her that even the scenes where I don't say anything, those are the scenes I'm really worried about because that's when I really have to do the acting because I don't have anything to express how I'm feeling—so I worked with her everyday . . ."

Beyoncé even dropped twenty pounds for the role. "I didn't want to recognize myself," she told *indielondon.com*. "I had the darker, big hair and looked different because of hair and make-up but I wanted it to be more than that. I was watching Diana Ross, Cher, and Twiggy, and everyone was so skinny back then. So I felt if I was wanting to be a fashionista in that time I would have tried to be thin. So I did it."

Reviews of the film were good, box office takings went through the roof, and Jennifer Hudson won an Oscar for Best Actress in a Supporting Role. As for Beyoncé's performance, some reviewers felt that she appeared detached as an actress but came to life when performing the musical numbers. This didn't stop her from gaining Golden Globe Award nominations for Best Actress and Best Original Song.

Opposite: The star playing the role of Deena in Dreamgirls *and (above) with her costars in the movie poster.*

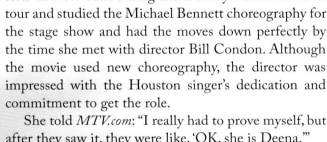

TINA TURNER

Starting in October 2008 and running through to May 2009, Tina Turner toured the world, playing more than ninety dates in forty different cities. Every night she performed twenty five songs, and every night the thousands of people in the crowd sang along with her. It was Tina Turner's 50th Anniversary Tour in celebration of her amazing longevity in the music business. Turner has been an inspiration for at least three generations of female singers and musicians thanks to her incredible persistence, stamina, positive attitude, and truly amazing voice.

Born Anna Mae Bullock in Nutbush, Tennessee in 1939, at the age of fourteen she was pressed into domestic service after her parents split up. At the age of seventeen she met a local band leader in St. Louis named Ike Turner, persuaded him to let her sing with his Kings of Rhythm, and so began her singing career.

Ike renamed Anna Mae Bullock Tina Turner, claiming to have found the name in a comic book. Together they enjoyed their first hit single, "A Fool In Love" in 1960. They married two years later and in between raising four children, recorded and toured together for almost fifteen years. As her autobiography (*I, Tina*) states their relationship was far from happy, and although Ike claimed in his autobiography that he "only" slapped her and punched her "without thinking," clearly he was physically, verbnally, and emotionally abusive.

Following her split from Ike, in 1976 Tina set about building a solo career. After a slow start, playing a Las Vegas residency and releasing rock and a disco-themed albums which flopped, in 1980 she acquired a new manager, Roger Davies (who managed Olivia Newton- John at the time) and began to build a spectacular solo career. After finding success in the United Kingdom after collaborating with BEF on "Ball Of Confusion" in 1982, she had a solo hit with Al Green's "Let Stay Together" from her album *Private Dancer* in 1983. The following year Tina broke the American market (again) with "What's Love Got To Do With It", from the same album, and never looked back.

Since then she has starred in hit Hollywood movies, had a successful movie made about her life, scored ten top twenty hit singles in the U.S., and sold millions of albums around the world. Named by *Rolling Stone* as "one of the greatest singers of all time," she has also been one of the world's top live performers, and even at the age of seventy proved to be an energetic, vivacious performer. It's no wonder that she continues to inspire world-class performers including Beyoncé, who jumped at the chance of duetting with her on "Proud Mary" at the 2008 Grammy Awards ceremony. Whether she looks forward to a 50th anniversary tour or not, Beyoncé clearly enjoyed having the opportunity to sing with a pop music legend.

> **"Turner has been an inspiration for at least three generations of female singers and musicians because of her incredible persistence, stamina, positive attitude, and truly amazing voice."**

Opposite: Beyoncé and Tina Turner in sparkling form at the 2008 Grammys.

SIX

I AM . . .

MARRIAGE

I N an age of instant celebrity access, Beyoncé's wedding to Jay-Z was shrouded in mystery and rumor. *People* magazine reported early in April 2008 that the couple had filed for a marriage license in Scarsdale, New York, which meant, the magazine said, that by law they would be tying the knot in the next five days. The reports were correct. A top-secret ceremony was attended by family and close friends, including celebrity pals Gwyneth Paltrow, Chris Martin, Janet Jackson, Jermaine Dupri, Usher, Wyclef Jean, Jennifer Hudson, and Jamie Foxx. The couple kept quiet about the event for the next six months. No photographs or interviews about the wedding were released and everyone associated with the ceremony signed confidentiality agreements promising not to talk about the superstar wedding.

Beyoncé finally discussed the union in the November issue of *Essence* magazine, explaining that she didn't need a special day since "it's been my day so many days already." She also said she had had no desire for an engagement ring because "it's just material and it's just silly to me."

Knowles was sure about their commitment to each other, and was adamant it was destiny that they would wed, saying, "We've been together for a long time. We always knew it would happen." Fans finally caught a glimpse of Beyoncé's wedding dress in 2011 when she included personal video clips in the music video for "I Was Here (Live at Roseland)."

The secrecy did cause some problems with friends and family, which concerned Jay-Z. He told Oprah Winfrey in a 2009 interview for *O* magazine, "The sad part is that we offended some. But people who love you understand. Because at the end of the day, it's your day."

It took a while for Beyoncé to publicly talk about her marriage, but she opened up in a November 2011 interview with *Harper's Bazaar* magazine when she said: "We have been together since I was twenty years old. We took our time and developed an unbreakable friendship before we got married. I admire his ability to inspire others. To me, Jay represents the American dream. I respect him so much; he is a great man and a great artist.

"We focused three years on our marriage and found that it brought us an even stronger bond and connection. But like anything great and successful in your life, marriage takes hard work and sacrifice. It has to be something both you and your husband deeply want. The best thing about marriage is the amount of growth you have because you can no longer hide from your fears and insecurities. There's someone right there calling you out on your flaws and building you up when you need the support. If you are with the right person, it brings out the best version of you."

Opposite: The golden couple watching a game of basketball in New York.
Above: Jay-Z and Beyoncé attending a fashion show.
Following pages: Performing "Single Ladies" on *Good Morning America* in 2011.

SASHA FIERCE

THE African-American community in America was naturally supportive of Senator Barack Obama's decision to run for president in the 2008 election. If he were to win, Obama would be the country's first African-American president, some forty-four years after the U.S. government passed the historic Civil Rights Act prohibiting discrimination based on color, religion, sex, national origin, and race.

Throughout election year 2008, Beyoncé was frequently seen wearing an Obama shirt as the Chicago senator hit the campaign trial. She said, "I'm really proud," according to Teleta.com. "I think we're making a lot of progress. It's an exciting time for my generation, regardless of whether you're African American or not."

In return, Obama told radio interviewer Angie Martinez that he was a Beyoncé and Jay-Z fan: "On my iPod, I've got a little bit of Jay-Z and a little bit of Beyoncé," said the senator. "A little bit of that stuff. I don't want to pretend that I know as much as my nine-year old or six-year old daughter."

Barack Hussein Obama was elected November 4, 2008 the first African American to ever hold the highest political, office in the country.

The election of President Obama affected Beyoncé on a deep personal level, as she explained to CNN's Piers Morgan: "My father, all of his history, he grew up in Gadsden, Alabama. And he was escorted to school every day because he was one of the first African Americans in his school."

Beyoncé cut short a promo trip for her new album *I Am . . . Sasha Fierce* to be in America for the celebrations. Ten days after the presidential election, *I Am . . . Sasha Fierce* was released as a double album. *I Am*, the first disc, featured introspective personal songs, while *Sasha Fierce* was crammed with beat-heavy dance tracks.

Sasha Fierce was a character Beyoncé had invented sometime before, to help her deal with stage nerves and perform without fear. She explained the mind trick to Oprah.com: "It's kind of like doing a movie. When you put on the wig and put on the clothes, you walk different," she said. "It's no different from anyone else. I feel like we all kind of have that thing that takes over. Usually when I hear the chords, when I put on my stilettos. Like the moment right before when you're nervous. Then Sasha Fierce appears, and my posture and the way I speak and everything is different."

While Sasha was a fictional invention, Beyoncé also wanted the album to be the most personal piece of music she had yet recorded. Again talking to Oprah.com, she said, "I wanted to reveal more of who I am."

On January 20, 2009, an emotional Beyoncé sang for the president at the Neighborhood Ball celebration following his official inauguration ceremony in Washington, D.C. The song choice was Etta James's "At Last" as the president and first lady danced.

She told *Good Morning America*, "I can't even describe to you how I felt. I'm actually right now fighting back tears because it's just so emotional. I'm just so proud of my country. This man was born for this. And he was born to lead us, and I just feel so inspired and so proud. I'm sorry, I'm so embarrassed. I'm just so lucky to be a part of this history. It's probably the most important day of my life, and I'm so grateful."

Opposite: The star in Sasha Fierce mode at the American Music Awards in 2008.

"SASHA

FIERCE

IS THE FUN, MORE SENSUAL, MORE AGGRESSIVE, MORE OUTSPOKEN SIDE AND MORE GLAMOROUS SIDE THAT COMES OUT WHEN I'M ON THE STAGE."

RARELY have a song and video captured the public's imagination like the first single from Beyoncé's *Sasha Fierce* album, "Single Ladies (Put a Ring on It)." Released as a double A-side with "If I Were a Boy," the song represented the more outrageous Sasha Fierce side of Beyoncé's musical split personality.

It's a bouncy, upbeat track that focuses on women's independence. In the second verse she gets to the song's memorable theme: if your boyfriend doesn't put a ring on your finger, dump him. The song was a sassy tribute to female empowerment. What's more, the track, and its accompanying video, were so instantly catchy with the fans around the world that the song went viral in no time, becoming part of global pop culture by the end of 2008.

When Justin Timberlake donned a black leotard for a spoof of the video on comedy show *Saturday Night Live* just a few weeks after the release of the record, it was proof that the song had taken on a life of its own.

With YouTube, a new and exciting Internet phenomenon, video has enjoyed a dramatic resurgence in the digital era. This time around it was in the hands of the consumer, mashing, remixing, downloading, uploading, and sharing. If something took hold in popular consciousness, it could spread like wildfire.

Some songs are forever associated with their videos. Michael Jackson's "Thriller" is an obvious example, Queen's "Bohemian Rhapsody" another. "Single Ladies" matched that feat with a video that started a global dance craze.

The retro-style video was filmed in just twelve hours in Brooklyn. Beyoncé chose to shoot the video in black and white, and the one-take performance video featured two dancers alongside the star dressed in a high-cut leotard. It was a dramatic look. Beyoncé used Bob Fosse–style choreography to interpret the sassy swing of the music and lyrics, and the dance moves were as catchy and doable as the song's insistent hook.

Beyoncé told BET's *106 and Park* show: "I saw this video on YouTube and it's three dancers and one of them is Bob Fosse's wife, who's this choreographer, and they're doing "Walk It Out" to the music. It's from the sixties and it's one take and it's black and white. And I thought, wow, how amazing would that be now because the videos have so many different cuts and takes, just to see a nonstop dance video, one take, all the way through. It was the most tiring thing I've ever done in my life."

"Single Ladies" won numerous awards, including Grammys for Song of the Year, Best R&B Song, and Best Female R&B Vocal Performance. It was Favorite Song at the 2009 Kids' Choice Awards and World's Best Single at the 2010 World Music Awards. The song gained more media attention at MTV's Video Music Awards—for not winning. When Shakira and Taylor Lautner presented Taylor Swift with her Best Female Video award, Kanye West leaped on stage, saying, "Yo, Tay [*sic*], I'm really happy for you and I'm gonna let you finish, but Beyoncé had one of the best videos of all time!" Kanye had jumped the gun. Beyoncé won MTV's overall Best Video award for "Single Ladies," as if there was ever any doubt.

Opposite: Beyoncé doing the now-world-famous dance from the "Single Ladies" video.

KATHERINE DUNHAM

The life of Katherine Dunham (1909–2006) offers enough inspiration for a nation of young, ambitious, and talented women. Best known as a choreographer who brought aspects of African dance into the American mainstream, she was also a civil rights activist, singer, and dancer who majored in anthropology in college at a time (the 1920s) when few females—and even fewer black women—entered the field. As she completed her degree, Dunham presented a paper to the Yale University Anthropological Club and had several articles published in academic journals, before heading to the West Indies to study not just the area's anthropological history, but also dance.

When it came to making a choice, Dunham's passion for dance and performance appealed to her more than the world of academia, so she set up the Katherine Dunham Dance Group. She included aspects of folk dance from Haiti, Jamaica, and Trinidad in her own work. Returning to America, to Chicago, in 1937, Dunham founded the Negro Dance Group. After working at a government-funded program for artists (the Federal Theater Project) she moved to New York to choreograph and star in live revues, which were so successful that she earned a part in the film *Stormy Weather* (1943), an all-black musical starring Bill "Bojangles" Robinson, Cab Calloway, and Lena Horne. At the end of the war she opened her own school, the Katherine Dunham School of Dance and Theater, in New York's Times Square. Well-known students of the school included Eartha Kitt, Sidney Poitier, Doris Duke, and James Dean, among many others.

Throughout the 1940s and 1950s, Dunham and her dance group thrilled audiences on Broadway and across the segregated South (where they regularly broke the Jim Crow laws), and influenced new generations of dancers and choreographers. Dunham also had a brief recording career in the 1950s, which couldn't replace the part that dance played in her life, as her health (knee problems particularly) prevented her from performing. As the civil rights movement gathered pace, Dunham was publicly, vocally supportive and took part in marches, arranged benefit performances, and—after becoming the Metropolitan Opera's first black choreographer in 1963, and President Lyndon Baines Johnson's technical cultural adviser in 1967—took her message to increasingly influential members of America's ruling class.

Dunham continued to tour Africa, South America, and the West Indies throughout her life, highlighting international affairs and problems that she felt America could help with. At age eighty-two she went on a hunger strike to highlight the plight of Haitian boat people and America's responsibility to them. Katherine Dunham made it not just okay but essential that African dance culture be understood and used by black American performers, whatever their genre. Beyoncé's use of African dance styles (and costumes) in her videos is a small tribute to the remarkable Katherine Dunham.

> **"Beyoncé's use of African dance styles (and constumes) and in her videos is a small tribute to the remarkable Katherine Dunham"**

Opposite: The remarkable Katherine Dunham in a studio portrait from 1946.

PLAYING A LEGEND

IN February 2008, Hollywood trade papers announced that Beyoncé had signed up to portray blues legend Etta James in a new movie about the 1950s blues and rock-and-roll era, *Cadillac Records*. It would tell the story of Chicago's Chess Records, the pioneering record label behind Chuck Berry, Muddy Waters, Howlin' Wolf, Etta James, and many more rock and blues pioneers. Oscar winner Adrien Brody was to play Leonard Chess, the owner of the record company that signed and promoted all these artists. Cedric the Entertainer was to take the role of blues singer Willie Dixon as the narrator, and Mos Def was to play rock-and-roll guitar innovator Chuck Berry.

Etta James, who passed away on January 20, 2012, started out singing in church, formed a three-piece girl group, the Peaches, and then went solo—a familiar tale, perhaps. Sadly, when James toured with Little Richard in the 1950s, the singer acquired a debilitating drug habit and struggled with a serious heroin addiction for years.

Determined to honor Etta James with as accurate a portrayal as possible, Beyoncé spent time in a drug rehab clinic in Brooklyn prior to filming the movie. She told Hollyscoop.com: "I never tried drugs in my life so I didn't know about it all. It was hard to go to rehab. I learned a lot about life and myself."

Beyoncé's schedule gave her only six days to film her scenes, an issue that concerned director Darnell Martin. She needn't have worried. Beyoncé, ever the consummate professional, arrived on set fully prepared. Darnell recalled to Cinemablend.com: "I only have her for six days—how is that going to happen? How it happens is, everything you imagine this glamorous, iconic, becoming-a-legend woman, what you imagine she must be like to be on set is absolutely not true. She is the most down-to-earth, sunshine in my life, wonderful, incredible, easy, brilliant, excited about working, tireless . . . angel."

Beyoncé saw the opportunity with this movie to play a more complex character, while still in the somewhat comfortable zone of portraying a singing star. She told the *Scotsman* newspaper: "For the first time, I was able to feel that out-of-body experience in a movie that I feel onstage."

The singer's next project and her first nonsinging role was as a wife and new mother opposite Idris Elba in the thriller *Obsessed*. The movie builds to a climactic fight between Beyoncé and the bad girl/stalker, played by Ali Larter. Unfortunately, Beyoncé's solid performance in her first straight role was lost in the reviews as critics lambasted the movie for its incoherent plot.

Commercially, however, the movie was a hit, topping the box office chart for its first week of release and becoming the second-highest-grossing movie ever for the film company Screen Gems. Everyone loved the no-holds-barred fight scene between Beyoncé and Ali Larter, which, Larter explained, were as real as a film ever gets. "We went for it like, 'You clock, I clock,'" Larter told MTV News. "A little head-butting, some kicks in there—we went for it. We got bruised up. We spent a week shooting it." The tussle won the MTV Movie Award for Best Fight in 2010.

Opposite: Beyoncé with Etta James at the premiere of *Cadillac Records* and (above) as Etta.
Following pages: The star performing in front of an image of President Obama in 2009.

"AT THIS POINT, I REALLY KNOW WHO I AM, AND DON'T FEEL LIKE I HAVE TO PUT MYSELF IN A BOX. I'M NOT AFRAID OF

TAKING RISKS

—NO ONE CAN DEFINE ME."

DESPITE her fame and her financial and artistic success, Beyoncé has never forgotten those less fortunate than herself, and her generous philanthropy has become a key feature of her staggering career. The Knowles family were among the first members of Pastor Rudy Rasmus and wife Juanita's St. John's United Methodist Church in downtown Houston. Rasmus began a Bread of Life program in the 1990s to help the most disadvantaged communities in the city, and the family were committed supporters from the beginning.

When Beyoncé and Pastor Rudy organized a food drive during her 2007 Experience tour, the lessons she had learned in church in Houston throughout her childhood were clear in her statement about the food drive: "Reaching out and touching lives is incredibly empowering. That's why I want my fans to experience more than my music this summer. I want them to experience the joy of making a difference by helping someone else."

Pastor Rudy told 39News in Houston that Beyoncé, who still goes to his church when she's in town, made good on an old promise. "She told me one day, you know, Pastor Rudy, one day when I make it I'm not gonna forget this church. And over the years she has honored that promise many times."

Beyoncé has helped people in many ways. Along with her younger sister, Solange, and Kelly Rowland, she was so affected by the Katrina disaster in 2005 that she started the Survivor Foundation with a $400,000 donation. The foundation has since given many millions of dollars to various Houston-based projects, including Habitat for Humanity, the Knowles-Rowland Center for Youth, and the Knowles-Temenos Place Apartments.

Beyoncé has not limited her charitable endeavors to her work with the Survivor Foundation. She worked with David Foster and his daughter in producing and writing "Stand Up for Love," the theme song for World Children's Day.

Furthermore, she donated her income from *Cadillac Records* to the drug and alcohol rehabilitation program Phoenix House. Then in 2010 she and her mother, Tina, opened the Beyoncé Cosmetology Center at Phoenix House Career Academy in Brooklyn, a substance abuse treatment program and a place to train in cosmetology to give those suffering from substance abuse a chance to turn their lives around. They pledged $100,000 a year to help the center.

Philanthropy is part of the deal with Beyoncé. She explained to *Self* magazine what giving back meant to her: "You don't do it to get praised. For a long time, being

> "REACHING OUT AND TOUCHING LIVES IS – INCREDIBLY EMPOWERING."

quiet about what I did was a conscious decision." And for anyone wanting to get involved, she advised starting close to home. "Think about what truly touches you and motivates you to help, then start locally. Once it's in your heart to give, you'll have to follow through. I am a happy woman—very happy—because I know that I've worked hard, and I love being able to give back."

Page 140: Putting on a show at the Grammys in 2009.
Above: Beyoncé teaching children in New York some of her dance moves.

CELEBRITIES have promoted perfumes and fragrances since the golden days of old Hollywood. Givenchy made a perfume for Audrey Hepburn back in the 1950s, and *Dynasty* stars Joan Collins and Linda Evans moved into the fragrance-selling business in the 1980s. However, it wasn't until Elizabeth Taylor launched her first fragrance, named Passion, in 1988 and then the hugely successful White Diamonds in 1991 that the celebrity-endorsed fragrance business became a billion-dollar industry. By the time Beyoncé's celebrity had reached a level where she could launch her own perfume, every major name in entertainment had already done the same. Jennifer Lopez, Sarah Jessica Parker, Paris Hilton, Jennifer Aniston, Britney Spears, Faith Hill, and Tim McGraw are just a few who have brought out perfumes under their own names, with varying degrees of success.

When she was offered the opportunity to produce her own fragrance with Coty, Beyoncé wanted to be hands-on and involved in every stage of the process. She told WWD.com, "Everything, from the bottle design to the name and the ideas for the commercials—that's me. When I commit to something, I do it 100 percent."

The result, named Heat, was launched in 2010 and sold for between $39 and $59 through department stores including Macy's. It sold outrageously well, with Macy's selling $3 million worth in February and March and seventy-two thousand bottles in one hour alone during Beyoncé's personal appearance in New York City.

Global sales of the perfume were also good. The publicity created when the United Kingdom's advertising standards body banned the steamy Heat commercial from daytime TV for the "sexually provocative nature of the imagery" only seemed to make the fans flock to buy even more.

At around the same time, sexuality would feature again in Beyoncé's next video release, her provocative collaboration with Lady Gaga on "Telephone." The pair had worked together on Beyoncé's "Video Phone," but this was Lady Gaga territory. The mini-movie video for the song was shot with a nod to Quentin Tarantino's 1994 film *Pulp Fiction*. *Rolling Stone* described the video as a "nine-minute-and-thirty-second mash-up of lesbian prison porn, campy sexploitation flicks and insidery winks at the two divas' public personas."

Lady Gaga loved Beyoncé's contribution, telling Ryan Seacrest on his L.A. radio show, "She was very courageous in this video. I mean, can you imagine me saying, 'Okay, now, Beyoncé, now you have to call me a very bad girl and feed me a honey bun'? . . . She trusted me because she likes my work, and she trusted me because she knew that I love her and that it's a mutual respect. It ended up being a masterpiece because she was so courageous."

Beyoncé in return was quick to express her admiration for her only real rival for the Queen of Pop crown. She told PrideSource.com: "If you took away every bit of costume and she just sat in front of a piano, she would still tear it down. She's just that talented, and she deserves it all. And I'm just happy to work with her. I love her."

Above: An advertisement for the singer's Heat perfume.

Lady Gaga opened the 2010 Grammy Awards at the Staples Center in Los Angeles with a rocking version of "Poker Face," followed by a stunning duet with Elton John. But it was Beyoncé who took home the most awards, picking up six trophies, with "Single Ladies (Put a Ring on It)" winning. She was in tears onstage as she accepted her trophy for Best Female Pop Vocal Performance on "Halo."

"This has been such an amazing night for me," she said—an amazing night, and a truly amazing five years since Destiny's Child split. Now perhaps she could take a little time away from the entertainment machine. "It's definitely time to take a break, to recharge my batteries," Beyoncé told *USA Today*. "I'd like to take about six months and not go into the studio. I need to just live life, to be inspired by things again. I want to go to restaurants, maybe take a class, see some movies and Broadway shows."

Above: A glowing Beyoncé captivates an audience in Brazil in 2010.

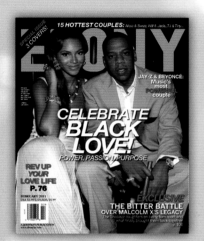

I N 2010 Beyoncé took a well-deserved break. Very few artists had worked as hard as she had for close to twenty years to get to the top. What superstar Beyoncé really wanted to do was have a normal life for a few months, as she later told Piers Morgan on his CNN show: "You know, I definitely enjoyed the simple things like, you know, driving and picking my nephew up from school. Traveling but not working and actually visiting museums and seeing ballets and having great conversations with people on the plane."

In what cannot have been an easy decision, Beyoncé also took the time away to consider her future, and in a surprising move she ended her business relationship with her father, Mathew. Beyoncé's publicist issued a statement from the singer that said, "I am grateful for everything he has taught me. I grew up watching both he and my mother manage and own their own businesses. They were hard-working entrepreneurs and I will continue to follow in their footsteps."

Choosing to manage her own career was not going to be easy, but she did have husband Jay-Z's all-powerful Roc Nation entertainment company to go to for advice. Although she had decided to take a break, there was still a new album to prepare for.

She told MTV News that she would cover a lot of new styles and sounds on the next record. "I'm not putting myself in a box, it's not R&B, it's not typically pop, it's not rock, it's just everything I love, all mixed together. It's my own little gumbo of music."

The album was scheduled for release at the end of June 2011, but tracks were leaked early on the Internet, leading Beyoncé to post on her Facebook page, "My music was leaked and while this is not how I wanted to present my new songs, I appreciate the positive response from my fans. . . . I make music to make people happy and I appreciate that everyone has been so anxious to hear my new songs."

The first single, "Run the World," didn't perform as well as previous songs, and critics were mixed in their response to *4*. *Rolling Stone* said it might be "her strangest record."

The *Los Angeles Times* said, "Taken together, *4* is a surprising, confident turn, even if the surprises are of a subtler variety."

In England, *NME* said: "Rather, there's the unmistakable sense of someone treading water, with even the OK bits here sounding uninspired. Not what you want from Beyoncé. Not at all. Let's hope her Glastonbury performance brings better memories."

On June 26 Beyoncé headlined the historic and prestigious Glastonbury Festival in England in a performance that would bring her great acclaim and win her many new fans around the world.

Above: Showing a different style on the cover of *Dazed and Confused* and *Ebony*.

Opposite: A beaming Beyoncé in 2011.

HOUSE OF DERÉON

LAUNCHING a fashion line with her mother was an obvious step for Beyoncé. Tina, after all, had been making outfits and styling Beyoncé and Destiny's Child since the very early days. In 2005, they launched the House of Deréon. The name came from Beyoncé's grandmother, Agnes Deréon, who had been a talented seamstress.

Instead of upscale couture, they opted for ready-to-wear but classy, affordable fashions aimed at women from the ages of eighteen to thirty-five. Jeans were priced at the $150 mark, with blouses going for $100–$150. Other pieces produced by the line included furs, bags, and shoes.

Beyoncé explained to *Cosmopolitan* that the idea for producing her own fashions dated back to the Destiny's Child years, when fans kept asking where they could buy the kinds of clothes worn by Kelly, Michelle, and Beyoncé. "My fans kept asking where they could get clothes like Destiny's Child's, so it was only natural for us to do a clothing line. I was adamant about not putting my name on something that I didn't love. I wanted to make sure it was true and honest and really something that we designed."

Beyoncé also wanted to draw on the resourceful creative techniques employed by both her grandmother and mother to turn something simple and ordinary into a piece of fashion.

"The whole theme is taking nothing and turning it into something because that's what my grandmother did with all kinds of fabrics. She just turned everything into masterpieces, and that's what my mother does," Beyoncé said in a statement.

In an interview with *Cosmopolitan*, Beyoncé talked about her own fashion icons: "Tina Turner is someone that I admire, because she made her strength feminine and sexy. Marilyn Monroe, because she was a curvy woman. I'm drawn to things that have the same kind of silhouettes as what she wore because our bodies are similar."

The clothing line was presented to the public on two major TV shows in 2005, *The Oprah Winfrey Show* and *The Tyra Banks Show*. The following year, Beyoncé and her younger sister, Solange, launched a budget House of Deréon line, called simply Deréon, with the snappy slogan "Where the sidewalk and catwalk meet."

Featuring more casual outfits but still with the trademark use of embroidery and appliqué, Deréon was modeled by Beyoncé, Solange, and members of Beyoncé's band, Suga Mama, in a series of print advertisements.

With the clothing business proving successful, Beyoncé and Tina took it global in 2011, launching the House of Deréon International Collection at Selfridges in London. In an interview with CNN, Beyoncé explained that much of her inspiration for the new line came from her experiences traveling the world over the past few years. She said: "I did a world tour, I traveled to Asia, Brazil, all over the world and I saw such beauty and my mother traveled with me and we decided we should mix these great cultures together and make something original and beautiful . . . you know, we have the mixtures of the African hair wraps and some of the Asian prints and we mix it with different textures, sequins, and gold jewelry and it just becomes very refreshing." The House of Deréon now also sells housewares including bed linen, and its continuing success looks assured with Beyoncé and her mother as joint creative directors.

Opposite: Beyoncé in a House of Deréon gown at the 2009 Oscars.

ROCK STAR

THE Glastonbury Festival in Somerset, England, is one of the United Kingdom's longest-running music festivals. Associated mostly with rock acts over the years, especially on its prestigious Pyramid Stage, the festival has rarely dabbled in pop and dance music.

Indeed, when MC superstar Jay-Z was booked for the festival in 2008, there was a Noel Gallagher–led outcry at the announcement. The Oasis guitarist told the BBC: "I'm sorry, but Jay-Z? No chance. Glastonbury has a tradition of guitar music. I'm not having hip-hop at Glastonbury. It's wrong."

Beyoncé was there when her husband walked out on stage carrying an electric guitar and, in direct response to Gallagher, launched into an acoustic version of Oasis's "Wonderwall."

"I have a sense of humor like a Brit, so I thought people would appreciate that. Noel Gallagher was one of the biggest detractors, so I figured that was a cool way to start the show," Jay-Z told MTV.

Beyoncé watched and learned. When she was talking about her own appearance at the festival, she explained, "I was able to see my husband perform here a couple years ago and it was one of the most exciting nights for me, and I don't know if I would have been asked to come if he didn't do the performance," she told the BBC's Lauren Laverne and Jo Whiley.

Beyoncé understood the importance of a good Glastonbury show to her career. It would be a milestone event.

"This really is the biggest festival in the world and I cannot wait to perform there. Everyone who attends is really appreciative of music and is in such a good mood that entire weekend," she said in a press statement. "I'm pumped just thinking about that huge audience and soaking up their energy."

Beyoncé, naturally, prepared diligently for her headlining performance. She asked co-headliners U2 and Coldplay for input on her set lists and spent three weeks in a London rehearsal studio, ironing out any kinks and wrinkles for the big show.

On Sunday, June 26, 2011, Beyoncé was the headline act that closed the festival. After two days of rain, the sun shone as she looked out over a sea of mud and screaming music fans.

"Glastonbury, I want y'all to know right now you are witnessing my dream," Beyoncé told the audience.

Her energetic hour-and-a-half-long show featured all the hits, including "Single Ladies," "Independent Women," "Halo," and "If I Was a Boy," as well as some crowd-pleasing versions of the Eurythmics' "Sweet Dreams," Alanis Morissette's "You Oughta Know," and Kings of Leon's "Sex on Fire."

"I always wanted to be a rock star and tonight we are all rock stars," she screamed.

Indeed she was a rock star that night, giving one of the finest, most accomplished sets the festival had ever seen. Sarah Carter of the *Guardian* newspaper watched the dramatic, high-energy show and wrote, "Beyoncé pulled off her show with such gusto and glamor that it will be unforgettable for those who witnessed it."

The festival set was a performance pinnacle for Beyoncé, as she told Piers Morgan the following day: "Well, you know, I'm still walking on the clouds. I'm still kind of shocked. I can't believe what happened to me happened yesterday."

Opposite: Beyoncé and the Suga Mamas wowing the Glastonbury crowd.

I AM . . . .

BABY BLUE

I N June 2011 in an interview with Piers Morgan for CNN, Beyoncé talked about the possibility of her becoming a mother. "I feel like I'm very aware of who I am. I feel great and I feel like thirty is the ideal age because you're mature enough to know who you are and to have your boundaries and your standards, and not be afraid, too polite—but you're young enough to be a young woman. I'm so looking forward to it."

It sounded as if Beyoncé was trying to tell the world something but wasn't quite ready to spill the beans. A couple of months later, however, she couldn't contain her news any longer. After singing at the 2011 VMAs, Beyoncé opened her coat, rubbed her stomach, and told the viewers, "I want you to feel the love that's growing inside me."

MTV immediately tweeted, "OMG Beyoncé just made a huge announcement on the #vma carpet! #baby!!!!!" and set of a twitter frenzy with some eight thousand tweets per second being registered around the world. It was a twitter record according to the technology review site C-Net.

Beyoncé and Jay-Z's daughter, Blue Ivy Carter, came into the world on January 7, 2012, at Lennox Hill Hospital in Manhattan. It was a major security operation, with Jay-Z and Beyoncé's organizations taking over a whole floor of the hospital and overseeing all the arrangements.

The couple released a public statement a couple of days after the birth: "We are happy to announce the arrival of our beautiful daughter, Blue Ivy Carter. She was delivered naturally at a healthy 7 lbs and it was the best experience of both of our lives. We are thankful to everyone for all your prayers, well wishes, love and support."

Family and friends were ecstatic. Beyoncé's sister, Solange Knowles, tweeted that the baby was "the most beautiful girl in the world," while Jay-Z protégé Rihanna tweeted: "Welcome to the world princess Carter! Love Aunty Rih."

To show his delight at the happy event, Jay-Z did what he does best and recorded a track to commemorate the birth of their child. For a pregnancy hidden in mystery, Jay-Z finally gave some insights in to the past nine months of his and Beyoncé's life. The songs talked about a miscarriage and Blue's conception in Paris. He proudly called his baby the child of a child from Destiny's Child.

Despite all the sentiment, Jay-Z and Beyoncé showed they still had a firm grasp on their business and brand, when three weeks after Blue Ivy Carter was born, they filed a claim with the U.S. Patent and Trademark Office, safeguarding her name.

Although taking time out to spend with baby Blue, it wasn't long before the consummate artist began talking about future projects. She had two albums of material to work on, a role in a new movie version of *A Star Is Born* (to be directed by Clint Eastwood), and a possibly a role in a comedy film from *Glee* creator, Ryan Murphy. If that wasn't enough, Jay-Z and Beyoncé began talks with Live Nation for a blockbuster world tour. A daunting schedule, perhaps, for anyone less driven than Beyoncé, the self-confessed workaholic.

Above: The new mother with baby Blue Ivy in an image released on a blog.
Opposite: The moment that Beyoncé announced her pregnancy to the world.

DISCOGRAPHY

Destiny's Child

ALBUMS

Destiny's Child (1998)
The Writing's on the Wall (1999)
Single Remix Tracks (2000)
Survivor (2001)
8 Days of Christmas (2001)
This is the Remix (2002)
Destiny Fulfilled (2004)
#1's (2005)
Mathew Knowles & Music World Present Vol.1: Love Destiny (2008)

SINGLES

"No No No" (1997)
"With Me" featuring Jermaine Dupri (1998)
"Get on the Bus" featuring Timbaland (1998)
"Bills, Bills, Bills" (1999)
"Bug a Boo" (1999)
"Say My Name" (1999)
"Jumpin', Jumpin'" (2000)
"Independent Women Part I" (2000)
"Survivor" (2001)

"Bootylicious" (2001)
"Emotion" (2001)
"8 Days of Christmas" (2001)
"Nasty Girl" (2002)
"Lose My Breath" (2004)
"Soldier" featuring T.I. and Lil Wayne (2004)
"Rudolph the Red-Nosed Reindeer" (2004)
"Girl" (2005)
"Cater 2 U" (2005)
"Stand Up for Love" (2005)

Beyoncé

ALBUMS

Dangerously in Love (2003)
Live at Wembley (2004)
B'Day (2006)
The Beyoncé Experience Live (2007)
I Am. . . Sasha Fierce (2008)
I Am. . . Yours: An Intimate Performance at Wynn Las Vegas (2009)
I Am. . . World Tour (2010)
4 (2011)

SINGLES

"Work it Out" (2002)
"Crazy in Love" featuring Jay-Z (2003)
"Fighting Temptation" with Missy Elliott, MC Lyte, and Free (2003)
"Baby Boy" featuring Sean Paul (2003)
"Me, Myself and I" (2003)
"Naughty Girl" (2004)
"Check on It" featuring Slim Thug (2005)
"Déjà Vu" featuring Jay-Z (2006)
"Ring the Alarm" (2006)
"Irreplaceable" (2006)
"Listen" (2007)
"Beautiful Liar" with Shakira (2007)

"Get Me Bodied" (2007)
"Green Light" (2007)
"If I Were a Boy" (2008)
"Single Ladies (Put a Ring on It)" (2008)
"Diva" (2009)
"Halo" (2009)
"Ego" (2009)
"Sweet Dreams" (2009)
"Broken-Hearted Girl" (2009)
"Video Phone" (2009)
"Run the World (Girls)" (2011)
"Best Thing I Never Had" (2011)
"Countdown" (2011)
"Love on Top" (2011)
"End of Time" (2012)

FILMOGRAPHY

Carmen: A Hip Hopera (2001)
Austin Powers in Goldmember (2002)

The Fighting Temptations (2003)
The Pink Panther (2006)
Dreamgirls (2006)

Cadillac Records (2008)
Obsessed (2009)
A Star Is Born (2012)

PICTURE CREDITS

The author and publishers have made every reasonable effort to contact all copyright holders. Any errors that may have occurred are inadvertent and anyone who for any reason has not been contacted is invited to write to the publishers so that a full acknowledgement may be made in subsequent editions of this work.

QUOTE CREDITS